FIRE YOUR

BROKER AND

TRADE ONLINE

FIRE YOUR BROKER AND TRADE ONLINE

Everything You Need to Start Investing Online

Jonathan R. Aspatore

McGraw-Hill
New York   San Francisco   Washington, D.C.   Auckland   Bogotá
Caracas   Lisbon   London   Madrid   Mexico City   Milan
Montreal   New Delhi   San Juan   Singapore
Sydney   Tokyo   Toronto

Library of Congress Cataloging-in-Publication Data

Aspatore, Jonathan Reed.
    Fire your broker and trade online : everything you need to start investing online /
Jonathan R. Aspatore.
      p.   cm.
     ISBN 0-07-135948-6
     1. Investments—Computer network resources. 2. Electronic trading of securities.
3. Day trading (Securities) 4. Investments—Information services. 5. Internet
(Computer network) 6. World Wide Web. I. Title.

HG4515.95 .A848 2000
332.64'0285—dc21

                                         00-035518

McGraw-Hill

A Division of The McGraw·Hill Companies

1 2 3 4 5 6 7 8 9 0   AGM / AGM   0 9 8 7 6 5 4 3 2 1 0

ISBN 0-07-135948-6

*The sponsoring editor for this book was Stephen Isaacs, the editing supervisor was Janice
Race, and the production supervisor was Charles H. Annis. It was set in Times Roman.*

Printed and bound by Quebecor World/Martinsburg.

McGraw-Hill books are available at special quantity discounts to use as premiums and sales
promotions, or for use in corporate training programs. For more information, please write to
the Director of Special Sales, Professional Publishing, McGraw-Hill, Two Penn Plaza, New
York, NY 10121-2298. Or contact your local bookstore.

This publication is designed to provide accurate and authoritative information in regard to
the subject matter covered. It is sold with the understanding that neither the author nor the
publisher is engaged in rendering legal, accounting, or other professional service. If legal
advice or other expert assistance is required, the services of a competent professional person should be sought.
—*From a Declaration of Principles jointly adopted by a Committee of the American Bar
Association and a Committee of Publishers.*

This book is printed on recycled, acid-free paper containing a minimum of 50%
recycled, de-inked fiber.

For the Pollocks and Aspatores—and a wonderful future of good health and happiness for our new family.

Disclaimer

This book is intended for educational purposes only. It is expressly understood that this book is not in any way intended to give investment advice or recommendations to trade stock or any other investment. The author and publisher assume no responsibilities for the investment results obtained by the reader from relying on the information contained in this book. Investing is inherently risky, and results obtained by some investors may not be obtained or obtainable by other investors in similar or dissimilar conditions. The reader assumes the entire risk of investing, trading, or buying and selling securities. The author or publisher shall have no liability for any loss or expense whatsoever relating to investment decisions made by the reader.

HOW TO USE
THIS BOOK

This book is meant to be your first step into the world of online investing. It is not meant to be a supplement for investment advice of any kind. We have supplied you with the knowledge of the best tools available to begin investing online today. This book is also accompanied by a web site that contains limited information from the book and will be a starting point for your entrance into the world of online investing. Take the time to learn about online investing—it is one of the most empowering tools to evolve from the Internet revolution.

CONTENTS

PREFACE

Whether you have been investing for years or are just starting out, online investing is appropriate for everyone. As an online investor, you pay lower commissions, have the ability to keep better track of your investments, and have access to more timely information and market research. This book will walk you through every step necessary to manage your finances online.

The Internet has revolutionized the way we do so many different things. From communicating with friends and family via email to making purchases online, the Internet has allowed us to take advantage of many new and exciting ways to enhance our lives. Online investing is just another basic way to take advantage of the Internet. This book will explain how easy online investing truly is.

Fire Your Broker and Trade Online walks you through the new generation of brokerage firms and provides you with everything you need to begin investing online. It also shows you detailed analyses of the different online brokerage firms out there and actual web screen shots so that you will be more comfortable when you access the sites. We even walk you through placing a complete trade online with several different online brokerage firms to give you a feel for each of the services. The growing number of online brokerage firms and different investment options available over the Internet allow you to make your portfolio as simple or as complex as you desire.

This book contains the most up-to-date information available for investing online. Regardless of your experience level on the Internet, we take you step by step from transferring funds into an online account and using specific online resources so that you take full advantage of the convenience and opportunities allowed by managing your investments online. *Fire Your Broker and Trade Online* is meant to help sort through the plethora of information available online and get you started in online investing today.

1

WHY EVERYONE SHOULD AND WILL INVEST ONLINE

THE REVOLUTIONARY POWER OF THE INTERNET

The Internet has fundamentally changed the way people conduct their lives in some way or another—whether they realize it or not. The most powerful aspect of the Internet lies in the fact that it is a tool that can be used by anyone with a computer and Internet connection. Almost every school now has access, proving that where we are today is only the beginning. Telephones are today what the Internet will be in only a few years. With Internet companies such as AOL, Amazon.com, and Yahoo becoming the likes of Ford, Coke, and General Motors of yesteryear, everyone needs to take notice. There are numerous ways to use the Internet to make your life bet-

ter. Investing online is one of the most powerful ways to take advantage of the Internet and take control of your finances. Online investing is empowering; it gives you the chance to access the same information as Wall Street professionals and put it to work for yourself. No matter what your experience with the Internet or online investing, this book walks you step by step through harnessing the power of these amazing tools.

THE INTERNET: WHERE DID WE COME FROM AND WHERE ARE WE GOING?

The Internet was originally created by the military as an additional means of communication should the country ever fall under attack. The Internet today, while certainly housing many military-oriented sites and content, is largely commercial, serving in countless ways for government, commercial use, and individual business and pleasure. Email has become the most popular mode of communicating for this nation's youth. Companies use the Internet as a giant billboard to promote and sell their products. Individuals play games, buy things, search for information, and display their art, just to name a few functions. What's coming down the road? As television and the Internet converge through the use of cable lines, there will be a day in the not too distant future when you will be able to sit in front of your television, watching the Masters Golf Tournament, and when the commercial for the latest Big Bertha golf club comes on, you can decide right then and there to purchase it. You may be able to use your remote to buy, at which point you will see a number of options to select (weight, male or female, color), and, once the specific product is selected, the television/computer will already house your credit card information so that your purchase is complete with no more than a click or two. But don't worry about this for now. Let's walk through the basics and make sure you are comfortable with everything else first.

New to you? An explanation of terms and such . . . Throughout this book, you will see a number of things that may be new to you or that you recognize, but you may not know exactly what they mean or represent. The first are URLs (uniform resource locators). These are addresses for things on the Internet, called web sites. An individual or a company buys or rents these addresses for very little (usually around $70 for two years). Much like your home address, URLs send a user to a place on the Internet. Just a change in one letter or a hyphen in a word can send you to a whole new web site. Virtually every brand is on the Internet, like www.cocacola.com (Coca-Cola), www.mtv.com (MTV), and even www.victoriassecret.com (Victoria's Secret).

Sometimes, it can be tough to get a specific URL; another company may already own it. For example, Delta Airlines has been unable to get the URL www.delta.com; another company reserved that address first, so Delta chose something a little different (www .deltaairlines.com). In addition, companies sometimes try to buy all URLs associated with their name. For example, Microsoft has purchased names that could give the company negative press, like www .microsoftsucks.com. It may seem funny, but there are plenty of people who might like to own that web address and put defaming remarks about Microsoft on it.

The most common Internet term is email, otherwise known, but rarely referred to, as electronic mail. Email is like sending a normal piece of mail electronically over the Internet. It is incredibly popular, not only because you can leave a person a long or short message, but more important it's free. People use it to send personal mail, businesses use it to send interoffice memos and external mail, and many web sites use it to keep users up to date and bring them back to the web site. For investment purposes, many financial web sites send email to let users know about new features on their web site (such as new customer service features or after-hours trading), to update them about their investments, or to even make them aware of an initial public offering (IPO). It is one of the best ways to communicate, and most email programs offer a filing system, so you can hold onto old emails for reference or accountability purposes.

SO, WHAT *IS* ONLINE INVESTING?

One of the most profound and immediate changes the Internet has brought is in the world of investing. No longer do individual investors have to make a phone call to their broker to buy and sell stocks. Nor do they have to visit their local "investment advisor" or "money manager" for hot tips. By the end of this book, you will be your own money manager and will be educated enough to know where to go to invest online, the advantages and strengths of individual online brokers, and the different investment options available to you online. And finally, you will be bestowed with an understanding of why, though you do not hold a stock certificate in your hands and you have never seen a brick and mortar office, your money is as safe and secure with an online broker as with any traditional brokerage firm.

Online investing is simply buying investments over the Internet. You do not need a broker. You do not even need to talk on the phone to anyone as you do it. There are several simple steps to this process:

1) *Have some money to invest.* You need a specific amount with most online brokerages, usually somewhere between $1,000 and $2,000 in cash or stock that you can transfer into your new account, but there are firms that specialize in bigger and smaller accounts. Details about this are discussed in Chapter 4.

2) *Invest with the best tools.* You need a computer, a modem, a telephone line, an email account, and an Internet service provider (ISP). For very little money you can get all of these if you do not already have them. These tools are further discussed in Chapter 2.

3) *Select a broker who meets your needs.* Some brokerages are oriented to the frequent trader; they have very low commissions but require bulk trades. Others target the average habits of most individ-

uals; they have higher commissions but provide access to much information never before accessible to the individual investor. More information on online brokerage firms is in Chapter 4.

4) *Do your homework.* You make your own decisions and have access to a world of information you probably never even knew existed. Research the buys you make. Keep learning. Invest intelligently. We discuss this further in Chapters 5 and 6.

WHAT YOU'LL FIND ONCE YOU GET THERE: INVESTOR'S INFORMATION ON THE INTERNET

The Internet is full of almost every piece of information you could ever need—especially regarding investing. You will find real-time stock quotes on almost all brokerage sites, as well as many online content sites, such as The Motley Fool (www.fool.com) and Yahoo! Finance (www.yahoo.finance.com). No need to get that dirty newspaper ink all over your fingers. And you won't need to call your broker or watch TV hoping to see your ticker symbol fly by to see how your investments have performed throughout the day. Now you can get all that information online. You can also get historical data for different stocks and mutual funds, with charts that map out how the investment has performed for any amount of time, be it the last two weeks or the last 25 years. You can access press releases and the most recent earnings reports, as well as find out when the stock last split. The information available on the Internet is endless. Consulting with other investors is brought to a new level online. Whereas you may discuss certain investment choices with your spouse, or seek the input of friends over dinner, online investment discussions are a whole new ball game. There are essentially two options: chat rooms and message boards.

Chat is like having a conversation, but you're typing your words instead of speaking them. It is done in real time: the moment you write something and hit <enter>, your words appear on a screen for the rest of your chat friends to see. There are countless areas that chat occurs online. Most portals, including Yahoo (www.yahoo .com), Lycos (www.lycos.com), and Excite (www.excite.com), have them. There are also specific web sites whose main focus is almost exclusively chat. Deja News (www.deja.com) and Talk City (www .talkcity.com) provide customer reviews on endless products and services. The options are truly endless. To start out, it might be best to visit a few different chat rooms on different web sites and "lurk." Lurking means you are "in" the chat room but you do not actually write anything; you simply observe. Lurking gives you a good sense of the kind of users that frequent the web site and the quality of the conversation.

Message boards are different in that they are not real time. You write a message, perhaps a question or a topic of discussion, and "post" it on the board. There are different boards for different things. On a particular site, there may be message boards for each individual stock, or one oriented toward beginners or people with a specific interest, such as investment clubs. You don't have to lurk on message boards; you can simply visit a site and read the different boards to get a taste of the subject matter covered. If you want to participate, you simply start a new string of posts or respond to one already there. For example, perhaps you'd like to know how people feel about a company's recent acquisition. You could title your post, "How does everyone feel about XYZ Widgets buying ABC Widgets?" Within an hour or a couple days (depending on how active a message board is and how interested the rest of the participants are in that particular stock), you will have several posts in response to yours, all with the subject line you used. It's a great way to get input from others and to feel a sense of community with other investors.

WHY INVESTING ONLINE MAKES SENSE FOR EVERYBODY

I don't belong online! That's just for _____. Fill in the blank: (a) hackers, (b) my kids, (c) guys who work at big computer companies.

Do you think people who invest online are particularly savvy with a computer, or have some secret insight into the stock market that average people simply don't possess? Guess what—they don't. They simply learned to do it, just as you will through the course of reading this book, and now they are comfortable with it. Put aside your preconceived notions. It makes sense for *every person* to invest online. You can do it at whatever level you feel most comfortable. There are countless options. Beyond just buying stocks, you can buy mutual funds, set up an automatic monthly investment program, participate in a direct reinvestment program (DRP) fund, or start an individual retirement account (IRA). It is a great place for people of every age and investor level to learn because there is a wealth of information available online.

The past few years have been a fascinating time for the stock market, and the advantages and insight the Internet offers makes now an exceptional time to start learning how to invest online. Research has never been this accessible, and trade costs have never been so low. Beginning investors have a world of information at their fingertips. This book offers not only information and URLs that lead to online brokerages, but also information about what resources are available online to help you make the smartest decisions with your personal investment goals in mind (these web sites are discussed in Chapter 6). This book does not tell you what to buy or even how to value stocks. Rather, it provides you with the most comprehensive and up-to-date information on investing online and finding the best online broker for you.

DIFFERENCES BETWEEN TRADING YOURSELF AND HAVING A BROKER

Brokers charge high commissions. They make money every time you place a trade, whether you buy or sell. Thus, it behooves them to recommend that you buy and sell often, even if it isn't in your best interest. First, you pay brokers commissions each time you do almost anything. Second, you may not know the companies they recommend you buy, and buying what you do not know or understand is never smart. Would you go to a store and buy sheets for your bed without looking to see whether the sheets are twin, queen, or king? Of course not, and neither should you buy a stock without first doing your own research. Let's be honest, your broker may not have your best interests in mind every time he or she makes a recommendation. Truth be known, with the advent of the Internet and the opportunities it provides individual investors, many brokers are pursuing and will continue to pursue new careers in growing numbers. The Internet has made many of them dinosaurs.

Certainly there will always be individuals who work within the financial industry, but the number of people who are brokers for individual investors will drop drastically in the coming years. Similarly, there will always be individuals who prefer to have someone else invest for them. However, online investing allows you to have the best of both worlds: you can do one or the other full force or a little bit of each if it makes you more comfortable. With the research you now have available at your fingertips, coupled with additional and sometimes more specific research from the online broker you select, you will be able to invest with ease and a strong sense of security and save money in the process. And that's what investing is all about, right? Saving and growing your money.

Advantages

- *Lower commissions.* As low as $8 a trade. No more paying a broker for bad advice or being forced to purchase 100-share increments.

- *Save time.* No "your call will be answered in the order in which it was received" or waiting in the uncomfortable chairs at the local branch of your huge brokerage firm where your dollars are an insignificant blip on its screen.

- *Taking your personal well-being into your own hands.* Why let someone else drive your Mercedes, or your Jetta for that matter? It's yours, and it should be fun. Enjoy the ride, and learn along the way. Only you can completely understand what your investment goals are and have your best interests in mind.

- *Current research.* Quotes, research reports, ratings, editorials from sites—it's all free. The information available to you online is the same as what the brokers use, no matter what they say.

- *Community.* Message boards and chat rooms provide a forum for sharing ideas and information.

- *Updates.* You'll be advised of the latest news via mail (henceforth to be referred to as snail mail) and email (electronic mail, free and fast).

- *Monitoring your current investments and watching for potential new ones.* Special email alerts notify you when a stock reaches a certain level.

- *Competition.* There are thousands of online brokers who want your account, and they will make it worth your while.

Disadvantages

- *You're all by your lonesome.* Remember that false sense of security we mentioned earlier? Well, there's no broker to blame if you make a bad investment; it's all you. But then again, isn't that empowering? Form an investment club if you want some form of company, or refer to your broker for specific circumstances that are beyond the scope of buying and selling stocks.

- *Time-consuming.* Although you do save money by not having to talk to a broker or a representative, you also need to do some homework with regard to the online brokerage you'll use and the investments you should make. Once again, however, this can be very empowering and often lead to many new investment opportunities you never even knew existed.

- *It's new.* The relative newness of online investing does not count as a true disadvantage, but it does deserve a mention. Anything new is scary to 99 percent of people. Well, let the Securities and Exchange Commission (SEC) put your fears to rest; the SEC carefully examines every online brokerage. And as for the Internet being a fad? Well, it's not. You're just going to have to trust us on this one. It's going to stick around for a long time and will eventually become as common as the telephone and television.

BUT WHERE DID IT GO?

Have you ever wondered whether a waiter who takes your credit card at a restaurant will jot down your number and expiration date quickly before bringing you back your card? Of course you do, we all do (at least those of us who understand that untold thousands can be racked up with those numbers through long-distance phone calls, mail order, airline tickets, etc.). Yet we continue to hand our cards over because we assume that if everyone else around us is doing it, it must be safe. Yet the same people who pass their card along to the waiter without a second thought have misgivings about taking that same credit card number and typing it into a screen on a web site. It's certainly understandable; very few people actually understand the technology behind web sites and where that information is delivered. The upside is that buying things over the Internet, whether stocks or cases of wine, is just as safe as any other buying activity. Shopping online, otherwise known as e-commerce, is a regulated practice, with specific rules in place to protect the consumer. Provided they know what to watch for, consumers can very easily safeguard themselves against fraud and the like online. In fact, in Chapter 2 we walk you through a checklist just to make sure you are set. How about the surveys they have all over Internet? Many sites offer users a chance to register on their sites, a practice that often offers users an opportunity to use sections of the site that are otherwise restricted. But what happens to this information you just entered? There was a lot of personal stuff in there, including your home address, your phone number, and even your annual income! Rest assured, there is a reason why many sites ask for this information, and once sent to them, it generally is in safe hands. This is one of the best ways online brokerages and online investing sites and can provide you with factual and handy information that specifically fits you. Security and privacy are discussed in more detail later in the book.

ONLINE INVESTING AND WHAT ROLE IT PLAYS IN YOUR TOTAL INVESTMENT STRATEGY

As we have mentioned already, there are a myriad of ways to invest online. You can use your online brokerage account only to buy and sell stocks. You may already have a 401K with your company. You could prepare for your retirement, set up a trust for your children, or put together an annuity for your parents. The point is, each individual is going to enter online investing at whatever level he or she is most comfortable. Still, some people, despite all the information available online for free, may opt to use an investment advisor for some or all of their transactions. For these individuals, having an advisor in the real world who has "been in the industry" for years is important. That is perfectly acceptable. Do not make fun of these people, and do not feel bad if you yourself are one of these people. Each investor is going to approach investing on the Internet at a specific level. We hope this book helps you to increase your knowledge not only of online investing but also of the Internet in general and how you can use it to make your life better. The key is to make the jump and enter online investing at whatever level you are comfortable with and grow from there.

WE HATE TO BURST YOUR BUBBLE, BUT . . .

In case you have been led to believe that investing online is the most brilliant and recent get-rich-quick plan ever, we're about to bring you back down to earth: it's not. It is simply a way to invest that will save you money, time, and hassle. There are no guarantees. A mutual fund you buy online may go down or it may go up, the same as if you were to buy it from a broker. The only difference is you will not pay high commissions, and you will be able to closely monitor it at any point in the day. You will be more educated as to whether to buy or sell, and you will have more resources available to help you make that decision.

WHAT INVESTMENT CHOICES ARE AVAILABLE

The choices online are the same as offline: mutual funds, index funds, DRPs, stocks, bonds, options, you name it. This book does not tell you what to buy, or what strategies to employ based on your individual needs, whether planning for retirement, paying for college, or buying a home. This book provides a clean, simply marked path to help you become more comfortable and confident managing some or even all of your money online. Let's face it, physical dollars cease to exist once they're invested; it all becomes numbers on someone's monitor in an office in New York. Why not get those numbers on your own monitor and grant yourself the privilege to see up close what's happening to your dollars. Brokers have had that privilege for years. It's time you got to watch your own money.

OTHER THINGS THE INTERNET OFFERS THAT YOU CAN'T GET ANYWHERE ELSE (OR AT LEAST NOT ALL IN ONE PLACE!)

You can customize some web sites to view only those items that interest you. For example, if you own six stocks and a mutual fund and want to watch a couple other stocks, you can put all of them into a customized area on many sites and go directly to that area whenever you visit that site. Makes those tickers of the past seem like a fond memory (or nightmare for those of us who, as beginning investors, tried to find one stock on the ticker while the names and numbers whipped by at light speed!). You can also bookmark favorite sites (your browser will have directions for doing this). To bookmark a site is to have a link to it, like having all your favorite books on the same shelf in the library. By bookmarking, not only will you not have to type in the name of the site every time you want to visit it, but you can also bookmark specific pages within the site so that you can skip to the stuff that really interests you. See how much time you're saving already? Most sites make it very easy to customize, and they hold your hand throughout the process.

BEFORE YOU START

Decide on your investment goals. Remember, this book is a guide, not a financial advisor. Sit down with your spouse, your investment club, your parents, or simply by yourself and decide what you want to accomplish. Once you've discovered these truths, you're ready to begin.

MAIN POINTS TO REMEMBER

- Everyone can invest online. You don't have to have a degree in computer science or finance to understand the fundamentals of online investing and how to make it work for you.
- Everyone can use online investing on a different level to enhance his or her investment goals.
- Investing online will not make you rich automatically; you have to do the same work you would do to invest offline in terms of research, selecting the right stocks for you, and choosing the right online broker for your needs.

2

ONLINE INVESTING CHECKLIST

Before you get started in online investing, it is important to go through a checklist to make sure you have everything you need. This includes physical items such as a computer and modem. More important, however, is whether you have outlined your investment strategy and examined your goals for investing online. If you are unfamiliar with the tools you need to get online, this chapter highlights each tool in detail and outlines some of the choices available, price points, and where you can purchase what you need to start investing online today! At the end of this chapter, in the online investing checklist, we take a close look at everything you should have ready before you start investing online, and we go through the security issues to give you complete confidence to begin investing online today.

HARDWARE

First is the actual computer. There are two choices in terms of computer type: an Apple Macintosh (Mac) and an IBM-compatible PC (personal computer). You may be familiar with Macs through Apple's recent advertising campaign for one of its newest models, the i-Mac. These are really the first "stylish" computers on the market and represent Apple's initial attempt to regain some of the market share Macintoshes lost to PCs.

Macintosh users represent less than 10 percent of those who use computers. Macs are great for people who use their computers for design work, as they undoubtedly have some of the best tools for artistic projects. One of the main reasons (and there are many) that Macintosh owns so little market share is the fact that it is not Windows compatible. By not being Windows compatible, Macintosh is less attractive to many users who enjoy Windows and/or who do not want to learn a new way to use their computer.

These days, i-Macs hover around $1,200 (and are available in colors such as grape and teal). These are great family computers, unintimidating for both kids and parents new to computers. Higher-end models, such as iBook and the PowerMac series, run a little more but provide you with more memory and speed.

IBM-compatible computers, or PCs, are the most commonly used computers. Despite the name, most PCs are not made by IBM. They are made by companies such as Dell, Gateway, and Compaq. These computers use Windows as their operating system (OS). Windows is a very user-friendly operating system, and many, once they have tried it, feel comfortable using it and do not want to change.

No matter which brand of PC you buy, all are compatible with the same software. Unless you work at a creative office (let's say a graphic design firm, a magazine, or an architecture firm, to name a few), your office probably uses PCs. There is simply more software available for a PC than a Mac (although much of the Mac software offers more details and amenities).

Because there are so many different manufacturers in the PC market, it's tough to give a simple price. The good part of this is that competition drives prices down, so PCs are generally more afford-able than Macs. A basic desktop PC, with standard memory and operating speed, will cost anywhere from $800 to $1,500. Add more memory and enhance the monitor features, and the price can go up to as much as $3,000 for a good laptop.

Where to buy a computer. If you're looking for a store to purchase a computer, check out stores such as Best Buy, Circuit City, and CompUSA. They often run specials, and the sales associates for the most part are fair at assessing individuals' needs and making wise rec-ommendations. Generally, however, the best bargains can be found online. Sites such as Computer Discount Warehouse (www.cdw.com), Value America (www.va.com), and PC Mall (www.pcmall.com) often have significantly lower prices than their brick-and-mortar counterparts. You can now also buy directly from the computer man-ufacturers, for example, Dell (www.dell.com) and Gateway (www .gateway.com). Nowadays you can buy computers in many different places, so be sure to comparison shop.

Laptop vs. desktop. Most likely you're familiar with both laptop and desktop computers. Desktops are the bulkier machines with big monitors you see sitting on desks at work. Although these models are slimming down, they are still not intended for travel. Laptops are the "cooler" contraptions you see people plugging away at on an air-plane. You can get virtually every amenity in either of them, so there is really no clear-cut winner. Laptops are almost always a couple hundred dollars more expensive, but the advantage is that they are portable. Buy based on your need. Do you travel a lot and find yourself on planes and in hotel rooms, wishing you could use your computer? Do you work from home exclusively? Laptops are undeniably smaller, and they get tinier (and more portable) each year. Some of the latest models tip the scales at 3 pounds and are less than an inch thick. Depending on which laptop you purchase, you also get a smaller screen than with a desktop PC. Since a monitor for a desktop is not limited by size, you can see a lot more and often get a better quality picture on a PC's monitor. PCs also usually come with a drive for both floppy disks and CDs, great for transporting work and doing research. These amenities often need to be added to laptops and have to be attached outside the actual body of a laptop, making their use much less convenient. There is also the issue of breakability with a laptop. Laptops are simply more easy to break by virtue of the fact that they're smaller and that you're usually traveling with them.

Whereas both options are great and really not terribly different from one another, to begin using a computer for general purposes, beginning with a desktop might be a better option due to lower price, slightly better ease of use, larger monitor, and durability. However, do whatever fits your needs better.

Speed and memory. Speed and memory are the biggest issues to wrestle with once you've decided on a PC or a Mac. The more speed and memory you get, the more costly your computer will be. Take time to consider what the computer will be used for and who will be using it. There are two types of memory: megabytes and gigabytes. Megabytes (MB) represent the operating speed of the computer. This affects how quickly your applications run and how many programs you can have open at the same time. Gigabytes (GBs) represent how much information, in the way of files, emails, and so on, you can save on your computer. If you are going to be using the computer for basic word processing functions and to get online, you need at least 32–64 MB and 2–4 GB of memory. But if you're going to be using the computer to create presentations and complex spreadsheets in addition to everything else, it might be better to opt for something along the lines of 128 MB and 6 GB. Keep in mind, you can add more memory, so you're not locked in for good. Just make sure your computer is upgradeable. If you have an old computer that does not have these minimum requirements, it may be a good time to invest in a new computer. Most older computers are too slow and have too little memory to allow you to take full advantage of the Internet.

Modems. Think of a modem as a translator. A modem takes the digital signals you put into your computer and changes them into analog signals so that they can travel over your phone lines. There are several different types of modems available at different speeds. The faster they can operate, the more they cost but the quicker your web pages will download off the Internet. Practically all new computers come with a modem. Many have internal ones installed, or they have external ones that connect to the computer. The most common speeds for these modems are 28.8 Kbps (kilobytes per second), and 56.6. You will be happier with the fastest Internet access you can get, without a doubt. Many service provides are now even offering T1, T3, or DSL services, which can be up to 1,000 times faster than traditional modems. Most businesses use these fast lines; however, for your personal online investing purposes, you will be just fine with a 56.6 Kbps modem—that is, unless you plan on getting into day trading, which requires a faster connection. When you hook up to the Internet, the information comes to you at a specific speed, mostly defined by your modem. Keep in mind that if you have call waiting, an incoming phone call while you are online may interrupt your session. If you plan to be online a lot, you may want to get a second phone line installed for the computer. This is a great option, particularly if you have kids who may be on the phone or online a lot.

INTERNET ACCESS CHOICES

To get online and use the Internet, you need a computer, a modem, an Internet service provider (ISP), and a phone line. Your ISP is what connects your modem to the Internet. ISPs are in hot competition with one another. Some of the largest and most famous players

include AOL, Compuserve, Earthlink, Mindspring, and AT&T.
There are even new competitors entering the field, such as NetZero
(www.netzero.com), that offer free Internet access. They make their
money on ads that show up in a little corner of your screen while you
are online. The costs for unlimited access to the web can range from
$15 to $25 per month (or much less if you use a free ISP). The best
way to find an ISP is through friends in your area. Ask your neigh-
bors and your friends who they use, what the costs are, and if they are
happy with the service they are receiving.

To use your ISP, you need a browser. The two leading browsers
are Microsoft Internet Explorer and Netscape. Both can be downloaded for free from their respective web sites (www.netscape.com
and www.microsoft.com). There are also some smaller players in the
browser field, including Opera, which runs well on slower computers. If you are using an older computer (and waiting for those dollars
to roll in from the investments you made online before you upgrade),
this might be a smart option for you (www.operasoftware.com).

Most ISPs you sign up with will give you an email account.
These accounts usually have the ISPs name at the end (like Jonathan
@aol.com or SuzyQ@earthlink.com). You can also get additional
email addresses if you like. Many of the portals, such as Yahoo
(www.yahoo.com) and Excite (www.excite.com), offer free email
that can actually be received by any computer with Internet access
because they are web-based instead of computer-based. To check
your email, you simply go to their web site and type in your password. Email is currently the most popular online application and provides a wonderful way to communicate with personal and business
relations, as well as receive information such as investment news
that may be of interest to you.

America Online is a national ISP, but truly different from the
masses in that it is a proprietary service. If you do not subscribe to
AOL, you cannot get into the service (there is a web site that anyone
can visit [www.aol.com], but that's a different entity and does not
contain the same information). AOL has the most members of any

ISP. It has local dial-up numbers in every area of the country (and much of the world). It grants you access to the Internet and your email account from anywhere in the world! Make sure whichever ISP you select has a local telephone access number. You don't want to be making expensive calls every time you get online! Make sure that the ISP offers competitive rates and that those rates are flat monthly charges rather than time based.

If you find this is not fast enough for your liking, which it is for 99 percent of the United States, there are other options your phone company may offer. An integrated services digital network (ISDN) can sometimes be added at a cost. ISDN lines deliver information much faster than a normal phone line. The downside is that it may not only cost more to install, but the per-minute charges and required additional equipment may make this option too costly for the individual user.

There is also some newer technology available in certain areas. Asymmetric digital subscriber lines (ASDL) work through existing phone lines, so there is no added expense or hassle. Another option, available through companies such as Excite@tHome and Road Runner, is high-speed cable access, meaning you get on the Internet through your cable lines rather than your phone lines. Currently this is available in certain areas only, but competition between these two companies is heated, and their expansion is moving rapidly. Call your local cable provider to find out if it offers these services. They cost about $20–$40 a month and are added to your cable bill. The difference in speed is incredible.

ONLINE INVESTING CHECKLIST

1) *Identify your investment goals.* What are you saving for? How much do you have to invest? What sort of growth are you anticipating? Whether you are planning to invest all of your money online, or just a portion, you want to identify the sort of investments you need to diversify your portfolio. It is a good idea to write down your

investment goals at least once a year, if not more frequently. This will help you clarify what you are saving for and analyze how previous investments have worked for you historically. It is also a good time to take a look at the other options available from various online brokerage firms to make sure that yours is providing you with the best tools to maximize your investment capital. Once you have identified your investment goals, you will be able to narrow your selection of online brokerage firms. Remember, though, that as your goals change over time, you may find that you require additional services.

2) *Identify what type of investor you are.* Do you make a lot of trades? Are your investment goals long-term or short-term? As an online investor, you can be as active or as passive an investor as you desire. Depending on your interest in the financial markets and the stocks you trade, there is a wealth of information available on the Internet for you to peruse and to make better informed investment decisions. The tools help you to monitor your investments once a week, have information sent directly to your email address when news becomes available, or allow you to even day trade. Again, one of the best parts of online investing is that you can follow any or all of these methods at any point in your investing career.

3) *Identify your comfort level with using the Internet.* If you are more of a beginner, you probably want to start with an online broker that has a very user-friendly web site and excellent customer service. Some online brokers are specifically geared toward more advanced Internet users and take the liberty of not explaining some of the basics of how their web site operates. If your understanding of the Internet is still minimal, do not worry (you are certainly in the majority). There are plenty of online brokers that can hold your hand through every step until you are comfortable to go it alone. If you have extensive experience using the Internet, then your main concern should be finding the online broker that fits the best with your investment profile.

4) *Identify the online brokers that fit your investment and Internet comfort levels.* In Chapter 4 you will see that we have labeled each of the top online brokers as beginner, intermediate, and advanced for

investment levels and ease of use. We have chosen only the top online brokers because there are definite advantages to being with more established firms. Narrow the list in Chapter 4 down to four or five choices and then spend some time visiting the web sites to determine the ease of use and services they offer.

5) *Determine what category of investments you are interested in.* Although we are only covering stocks in this book, there are numerous other securities that you can invest in online, including options, bonds, and foreign stocks. Not all online brokerage firms offer the ability to trade these securities. If you think that such investments may be of interest to you in the near future, seek a broker that offers them. However, because these investment options are for more advanced traders, most online brokerage firms for beginners do not offer them. It is very easy at a later point to open an additional account with another online broker. Just as they like to diversify their investments in different types of stocks, many online investors like to have accounts at different online brokers in order to take advantage of the special features at each, such as initial public offerings (IPOs) or after-hours trading.

6) *Make sure that each of these candidates is insured.* Discount brokers are covered by the same government-sponsored Securities Investment Protection Corporation (SIPC) as full-service brokers; their accounts are insured up to $100,000 in cash and up to $400,000 in other assets. Each online broker should be insured by the SIPC. If a broker is not, don't even consider it.

7) *Look for special offers.* Numerous online brokers offer special deals such as a certain number of free trades, $75 cash, or even airline miles. The competition among online brokerage firms is fierce, so be on the lookout for special offers that will make it worth your while.

8) *Read the fine print.* Although an online broker may have the lowest cost per trade, there may be hidden costs that in the long run make that firm more expensive. For example, online brokers sometimes charge for wire transfers, account transfers, and electronic transfers; there may also be inactivity fees and special handling fees. The chart

in Chapter 4 gives you most of the information on the top online brokers, but always be on the lookout for other charges that make your transactions more expensive. In addition, almost all of the online brokers have minimum opening balances. The best way to determine the lowest fees is to add up what you think will be the total annual cost of your transactions. Remember, however, that price is just one component of choosing an online broker.

9) *Check on their customer service.* Excellent customer service is often overlooked but is worth its weight in gold when you have a problem. Sometimes online brokers that charge the lowest fees can afford to do so because they spend less money on hiring people in areas such as customer service. Particularly if you are just getting started with online investing or the Internet in general, customer service may be the most important criterion when choosing an online broker. A good customer service rep should be able to walk you through every step of placing a trade and answer any general questions you may have, either via email or preferably over the phone. It is a good idea to call each customer service department to make sure the person you are speaking with actually knows what he or she is talking about. Also, before you accept any help, make sure you will not be charged higher commissions for the help you receive.

10) *Managing your account.* Another important criterion is the ability to manage your account effectively. An online broker should be able to present you with all of the information you need to research stocks or find out breaking news. It should even allow you to customize your page in order to have all of your specific information available each time you log in. With the overabundance of information present on the Internet, the ability of an online broker to present you with information in a clear and concise manner is very important. In addition, some online brokers will present for you all of the documents you need for tax purposes and keep an updated copy throughout the year. It is a good idea to ask for a temporary account name and password to see how well the information is presented on the site before you sign up.

11) *Opening an account.* Now that you have experimented with the finalists, you are ready to make the jump to deciding on the winner(s). We walk you through every step of this process—screen by screen—in Chapter 3. Remember, many people have accounts with more than one online broker in order to take advantage of special opportunities offered by each firm. In addition, it is very easy to switch firms or liquidate an account in general—one phone call should be all it takes. It really does not matter if you are investing $1,000 or $100,000: opening an account is very easy. Remember, online investing allows you to buy anywhere from 1 to 1 million shares in a single transaction. To open an account, you will usually be required to fill out part of the form online, then the broker will send the remaining parts to be signed. It usually takes anywhere between three and five weeks before your account is credited with funds; however, you will usually have access to the special features on the web site as soon as you sign up.

12) *Funding your account.* Once you have decided which online broker is best suited for your needs, it is time to get your account up and running. After you have filled out the account information online, the broker will usually provide you with the necessary information to start accessing some of its special features. However, you will not be able to actually place a trade until you have funds in your account. Usually this involves sending the broker a check, wiring money from an existing bank account, or transferring stocks from a different brokerage firm. The process is very easy. If you are uncomfortable with any aspect of it, call the customer service department to clear up any questions. It usually takes at least a week or two and occasionally longer for the funds or stocks to be successfully transferred to your new account. This is a good time to be experimenting with your new online broker, who should have some sort of simulation or practice accounts you can use to get the feeling of making trades and managing your account. It is always a good idea to get a good understanding of how everything works before you start trading for real. This is a great time to experiment because as soon as you see the funds in your account, you will be ready to start online investing.

13) *Start investing.* Now that your account is funded, it is time to invest your money. Every day that your funds sit idle in your account is another day that you could be gaining interest. Although it is never a good idea to make a rash investment decision, you should be ready to put your hard-earned dollars to work as soon as they become available. By this point you should have done some researching and have an idea which stocks you may be interested in purchasing. Online investing makes placing trades easier than ever before. Once you get started, you can continue to explore all of the amazing opportunities online investing provides.

14) *Get in the habit of managing your account.* Once you have started investing, it is important to get in the habit of managing your account on a regular basis. Online investing is an empowering tool for the individual investor; the investments do not happen automatically nor does the account care for itself. Because you are now your own broker, it is important to get in the habit of following your investments and researching new opportunities on a weekly, monthly, or even quarterly basis. The Internet makes managing your account easier than it has ever been, and with the dozens of sites devoted to personal finance, there are numerous ways to stay on top of the markets. By actively managing your account, you will be able to monitor your investments and decide when it is time to buy, sell, and invest in other opportunities.

SAFETY TIPS

Although there have been amazing strides made in online security, it is a good idea to still be cautious. Remember, there are just as many security issues when investing with a traditional broker, so don't be deterred by concerns of online safety. Fortunately, online investing is one of the most heavily regulated forms of e-commerce. Every day the SEC makes sure licensed online brokers are doing business by the book and that they are providing a secure experience for their investors. Although most online brokers are insured for online fraud, you will make your investment experience that much more safe if you follow these steps:

- *Read the fine print when submitting information.* Make sure that your information is kept strictly private and the broker will not disclose any of it to a third party.

- *Create unique user names and passwords.* As easy as it may be to remember your wife's or mother's maiden name as a password, this is very easy for other people to figure out. Create user names and passwords that combine upper- and lower-case letters, numbers, and symbols to ensure a higher level of security.

- *Turn off the "cookies" setting on your computer.* A cookie is a way for a web site to keep track of your patterns when you visit the different areas on the site. All computers have the ability to turn off the cookies setting.

- *Make sure that you are using a secure server.* All online investment firms should offer a secure server for making trades and sharing personal information. Make sure your firm has ways to ensure the privacy of the information you are submitting.

- *Avoid sending private information in an email.* It is always a good idea not to send account numbers, user names, or passwords via email. Keep this information private, and do not email it to anyone.

By following these simple steps, you can greatly reduce any chances for online fraud. Online investing is just as safe as investing with a traditional broker, perhaps more. Still, it does not hurt to be careful. Individuals have been investing online now for over three years, and the online investing firms are well equipped to ensure a safe and friendly environment.

MAIN POINTS TO REMEMBER

- To get online, you need a computer, a modem, an ISP, and a telephone line.

- Make sure your computer has the minimum operating capacities that will allow you to take full advantage of the Internet and online investing.

- Investing online is just as safe as investing with your traditional broker as long as you follow the few simple steps described in this chapter.

3

OPENING AN ACCOUNT ONLINE

OPENING AN ONLINE ACCOUNT

Opening an account with an online brokerage firm is relatively easy. Many times you can fill in most of the application online, print it out, and then sign it and send the material in. The process may require some information to be completed online followed up by forms snail mailed to the customer for signature, and the deposit mailed back to the broker. The forms are almost identical to what you would fill out if you were working with a traditional broker. You will almost always be asked to provide the following information, so make sure you have it available when you are ready to open your account:

General information

Name of Account Holder or Joint Account Holders

Address

City, State, Zip, Country

Daytime and Evening Phone Numbers

Email Address

Date of Birth

Social Security Number

Gender

Marital Status

Number of Dependents

This boilerplate information should be readily accessible. If you are a citizen of a country other than the United States, you will have additional information to fill out. Otherwise you should be able to quickly move on to the next section.

Occupational information

Employment Status

Employer Street Address

Identify any publicly traded company that you or a member of your household is affiliated with.

Do you hold any NASD licenses?

The occupational information section is meant to make sure that you are not directly affiliated with any publicly traded companies or that you do not currently own more than 10 percent of any publicly traded company. Because individuals who are directly affiliated with publicly traded companies can trade their shares of stock only during certain time periods, there are specific restrictions that must be placed on their accounts. All applications will also have a blank to fill if you are not currently employed or are a student, homemaker, or if you are retired.

Banking information

Money Fund Instructions (Select a type of municipal or money market portfolio)

Banking Reference Information (Bank Name, Branch, City, Country, Account Number)

Investing Experience (Stocks, Options, Mutual Funds, Bonds)

Investment Objectives (Growth, Tax Deferral, Current Income, Liquidity, Speculation)

Financial Information (Annual Income, Liquid Net Worth, Net Worth Excluding Home, Estimated Tax Bracket)

The banking information section is for the online broker to be able to determine your investment profile. In addition to providing banking reference information, you are informing brokers of your investing experience and objectives, which they will use to help you in various ways. For example, when calling or emailing customer service they will be able to determine the best way to explain a situation or event to you. In addition, it is very important to identify your money fund instructions. Your money fund instructions inform the online broker about the type of account that should hold your cash. Most online brokerage firms offer different municipal trust and money market portfolios, or you can just leave it in cash. However, the risk in these types of portfolios is little more than the cash sitting in your bank account and you can usually earn 50 percent more interest.

User name and password

User Name

Password

Mother's Maiden Name

Question and Answer (in case you forget your password)

Remember to choose a unique user name and password. Although online brokerage firms employ significant measures to deter fraud and have insurance as well, it is a good idea to choose a user name and password that are nonsensical. The best way to do this is to use a combination of upper and lower case letters and numbers.

Additional information

Additional Parties (Joint Accounts)

Other

The information on each online brokerage firm's application will be a little different. However, all firms will ask you for the bulk of information discussed here. Get your material together so that you can make this process as quick and painless as possible. After you have filled out the form, it is time to transfer the funds and begin investing online.

TRANSFERRING FUNDS

Almost all online brokerage firms require you to have a minimum amount of stock or cash in your account. Therefore, you will be required to either transfer securities into your new account or send in a check that you can then use to purchase securities.

Transferring securities

Account Number Where Securities Are Currently Being Held

Account Number at New Online Brokerage Firm

Wiring Instructions for New Online Brokerage Firm

Exact Amount and Identity of Securities Being Transferred

Transferring securities involves calling the company where your securities are currently held and providing the company with some specific information. You will be required to have your new account number and wiring instructions. You can obtain this information by calling or emailing your new online broker. Then, it is a good idea to let your new online brokerage firm know the exact amount and securities that are being transferred over. The transfer may take anywhere from two days to two weeks. Make sure to ask your old company about, and advise your new broker of, the anticipated timing for the transfer.

Sending a check

Check for Minimum Balance Required at Online Brokerage Firm

Address Where Check Should Be Sent

If you are sending in a check, it is very easy to write a personal check from your bank account and send it in. It is also a good idea when sending in a check to make sure the funds will be in some form of an interest bearing account. Most online brokerage firms offer money market funds where you can be earning anywhere from 2 percent to 4 percent depending on the type of fund.

Additional information

Country of Origin for Securities or Cash

Citizenship

Although transferring funds into your new online account is relatively easy, the funds will be posted to your account in the timeliest manner and you will be able to access your account much sooner if you provide all of the information requested. People who forget to include information about their citizenship and the origin of their securities or cash may delay their account being opened. Make sure you provide all of the preceding information in order to expedite the process. Figures 3-1 through 3-5 show us the steps to open an account on Ameritrade. Although the procedure varies a bit from one

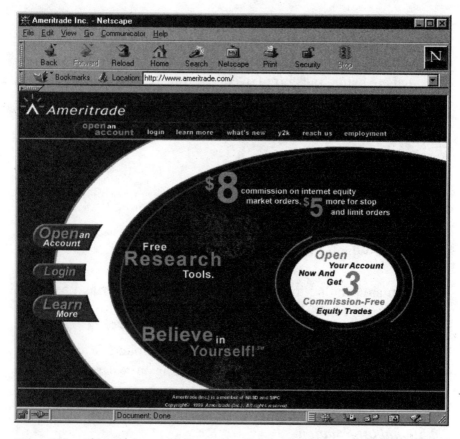

Figure 3-1.   This is the home page for Ameritrade. From this page you can perform a variety of functions, including opening an account. *(Courtesy of Ameritrade)*

online broker to another, these screens are a good representation of what you can expect.

ACCESSING YOUR ACCOUNT

Almost all online brokers have areas on their web site that are free to both account and non-account holders and that can be used for research on the market and particular stocks. It is a good idea to

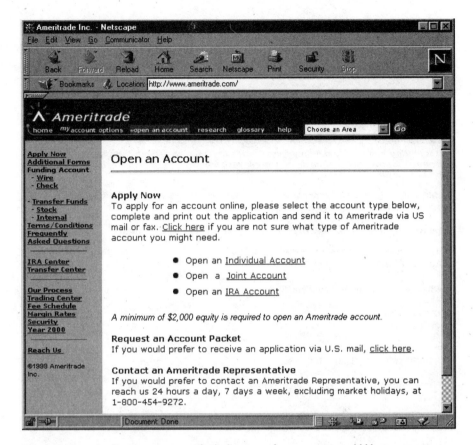

Figure 3-2.   On this page you are asked what type of account you would like to open. An individual account is the one you want if the account is just for you. Select a joint account if the account is for you and another individual, such as a spouse. An IRA is an entirely different type of account. Figures 3-3 through 3-5 show an individual account, although opening a joint account is virtually the same. To open an IRA, you will need almost the identical information, but the agreements will be different. *(Courtesy of Ameritrade)*

begin getting comfortable navigating the site and learning about the wealth of information that your online broker provides. Keep in mind that some online brokerage firms will not activate your account until you have transferred the funds. It is also a good time to begin experimenting with a "pretend" portfolio if your online brokerage firm offers such a service.

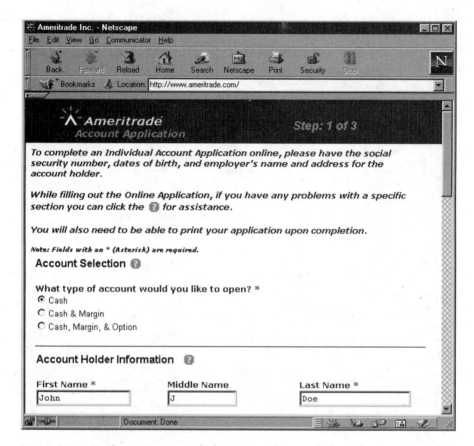

Figure 3-3. On this page you are asked to enter your personal information. In addition, you must decide what type of account you would like to open. A cash account is the standard account that most investors open initially. You can always go back later and add the other options to your account. *(Courtesy of Ameritrade)*

When accessing your account, you will usually need just your user name and password, which should have been assigned to you when you registered. Most online brokers also have a customer service department that can answer any questions you may have and help you to retrieve your user name and password information should you misplace or forget it.

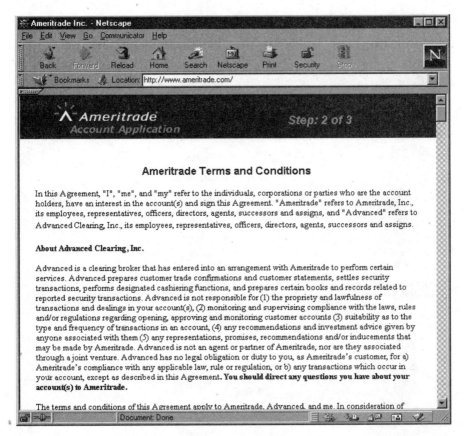

Figure 3-4. The Ameritrade Terms and Conditions page represents the type of standard agreement that all brokers require their customers to sign. Although it is a bit different from one online broker to another, all of the top firms stipulate very similar conditions. If something looks strange in the agreement for any online broker, do not hesitate to call and see if other online brokers do the same. *(Courtesy of Ameritrade)*

THE MECHANICS OF PLACING A TRADE

Placing a trade online is actually easier than placing a trade with your broker. Your online brokerage firm is available at all times to provide you with execution and breaking news that can assist you. Keep in mind, however, that most online brokers advertise their price for trades as simply a market order (buy at current market price). Other

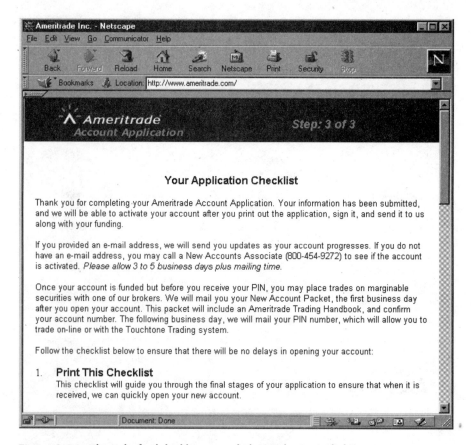

Figure 3-5. This is the final checklist page, which provides you with the necessary information to ensure that your account is opened in the timeliest manner possible. You are now ready to start placing trades with your new online brokerage as soon as it has received your check and officially opened the account. *(Courtesy of Ameritrade)*

transactions can cost a little more, so it is important to read the fine print on the fees table. When placing a trade, you will need the following information:

User Name

Password

Transaction (Buy, Sell, Sell Short, Buy to Cover)

Stock Symbol

Price (Market, Limit, Stop, Stop Limit)

Number of Shares

Term (Good for Day, Good Until Canceled)

You basically have four options when placing your trade: buy, sell, sell short, buy to cover. Buying and selling stocks are very straightforward.

- *Selling short* means that you are selling a security that you do not own.
- *Buy to cover* means that you are buying back a stock that you had previously sold short.

In most online brokerage firms you must be approved for these types of transactions because it is considered a much riskier investment option. Once you have indicated your action, it is time to identify the stock symbol and determine the price you are willing to pay.

The stock symbol can be obtained on the web site of your online broker. Almost all have an option that allows you to type in the name and it will respond with the appropriate ticker symbol. It does not matter which U.S. exchange the stock is on; your online broker will automatically take care of that. If you do not want to exit the screen you are in, you can always open another window with your browser and go to another site for the appropriate ticker symbol.

There are generally four ways to indicate the price you are willing to pay for a security: market, limit, stop, and stop limit.

- A *market order* means that you are going to buy or sell at the best price available at the time the broker receives your order that day.
- A *limit order* means that the broker will only buy or sell the security if the price is at a specified price or better. A limit order

can be placed as good-till-canceled (GTC) or as a day order (explanations for GTC and day orders follow).

- A *stop order* is used to buy or sell a security once it reaches a set price. For a buy stop, you enter a price above the current price that you want to buy at; a sell stop is at a price below the current bid price.

- A *stop limit* is when the stop price is reached or has passed on a limit order. If a stock trades past a stop limit, the transaction will not take place until the limit price is reached.

Most online brokers allow you to choose any number of shares to trade. If you are trading over 5,000 shares, most online brokers begin charging you a fee above the normal trade charge. Simply fill in the number (making sure you have enough cash in your account to cover it) and press <enter>. You will usually be asked to confirm all of the information again before your trade is confirmed.

You will always be asked to identify the time limits on your orders. The basic ones are day, good-till-canceled (GTC), good-till-executed (GTX), immediate or cancel, fill or kill, at open, and at close.

- A *day order* means that the trade is valid only for the current day; it expires as of the close of the market that day. Most brokers classify all orders as day orders unless otherwise specified.

- A *GTC order* is valid until it is canceled or executed; most online brokers will allow a GTC order to last for approximately 90 days. A *GTX order* remains in effect until it is executed; these may also be used for crossing sessions on listed exchanges that operate between 4:15 P.M. and 5:00 P.M. Eastern Standard Time.

- An *immediate or cancel order* means that the order is to be executed immediately or otherwise canceled. It is important to consider that this type of order may result in a partial execution of the order with the other part being canceled. The way to avoid this is by identifying it as a fill or kill order.

- A *fill or kill order* is executed immediately in its entirety or otherwise canceled.

- An *at open* order simply means the broker should try and execute the order as close to the open of the trading day (9:30) as possible.

- An *at close* order simple means that the trade should be executed as close to the end of the trading day as possible (4:00).

- In addition, some online brokers will allow you to specify if an order should be an all-or-none (AON) order or a do not reduce order. An *AON order* is for transactions over 100 shares in which you specify that you want all the shares to be executed at the same time or not at all. *Do not reduce orders* are limit orders to buy, stop limit orders to sell, or stop orders to sell that are not lessened by the amount of an ordinary dividend on the ex-dividend date.

In Figures 3-6 through 3-20, we take a look at placing a trade and various other services on a few of the top online brokerage firms.

Figure 3-6. This is the main page of Datek. From here you can easily log in by clicking on the "login" button in the upper left-hand corner. The same options are available on the rest of the page. *(Courtesy of Datek Online)*

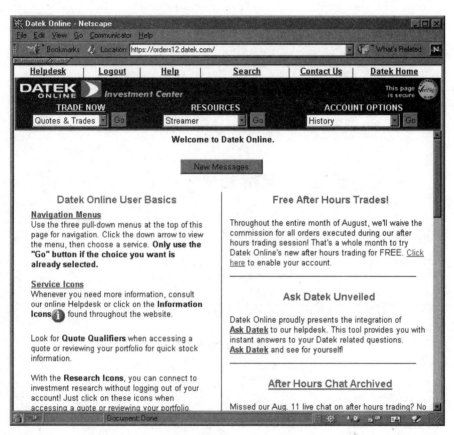

Figure 3-7. Now that you have successfully entered the login, you are ready to click on the "go" button in the upper left-hand corner of the screen so that you can place a trade. Note that there are numerous other options you can pursue here if you want to do additional research before you place your trade or see how the market is doing that particular day. *(Courtesy of Datek Online)*

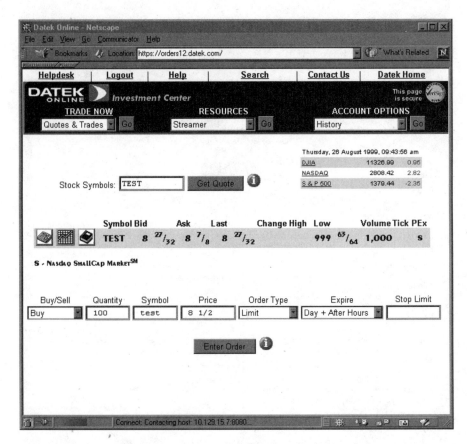

Figure 3-8. You have to indicate certain details about your order. Remember that at any point you can abort and do more research if you are uncomfortable with or unsure about any feature. You can also call Datek's customer service number to get some additional assistance if you are still uncomfortable placing your first couple of trades. Remember, once you click on the "enter order" button, you will still have a chance to finalize your trade before it is official (specifically on Datek). *(Courtesy of Datek Online)*

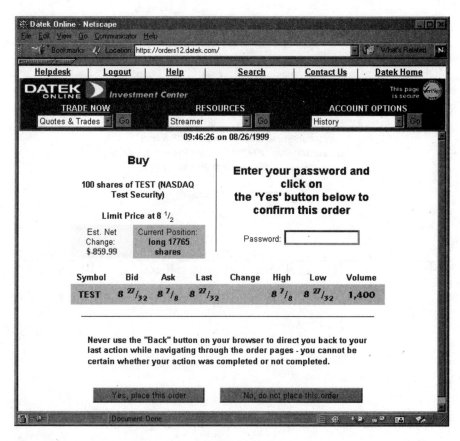

Figure 3-9. This is the final screen confirming the information you have entered regarding the trade. Once you hit the "Yes, place this order" button there is no undoing the transaction. Make sure to double-check the details on the left-hand side before hitting the button. *(Courtesy of Datek Online)*

45

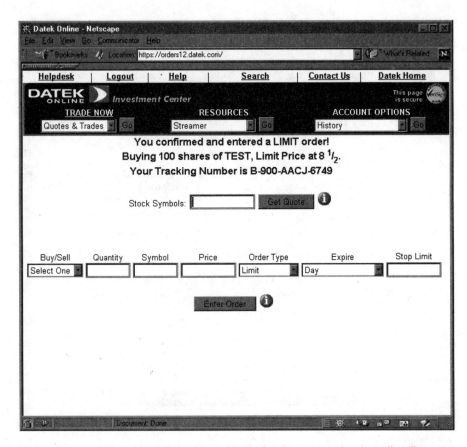

Figure 3-10. This screen confirms that your order has been received and usually will appear within a couple of seconds after you have placed the trade. Remember, it can take minutes or even hours sometimes to fill a trade depending on order type. Datek provides you with a tracking number so that you can follow up on your trade. You will receive another confirmation once the transaction has been completed. The screen resets and you are ready to place another trade if you so desire. *(Courtesy of Datek Online)*

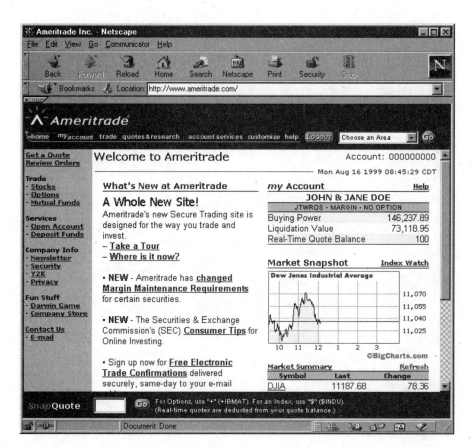

Figure 3-11. This is the first screen you see once you have successfully logged into the Ameritrade web site. It gives you a quick overview of your account balances, as well as a market activity snapshot. Ameritrade also uses this area to inform its customer about new features and other information. Navigation to the various sites within the Ameritrade site is accomplished by using either the side menu bars, the top menu bars, or the pull-down menu at the upper-right corner. *(Courtesy of Ameritrade)*

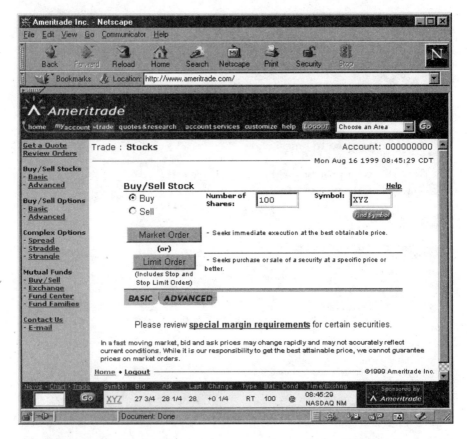

Figure 3-12. By using the side menu, the top menu bar, or the drop-down menu, you can get to the trading page. The Ameritrade trading page gives a basic and advanced order ticket. The basic ticket, shown here, is very simple and intuitive. Click on the button marked "Buy" or "Sell," enter the number of shares and the stock symbol, and indicate whether the order is a market or limit order. If a market order, the customer is taken to a readback screen (Figure 3-13). If a limit order is chosen, another screen allows the customer to enter the limit, stop, or stop-limit price before going to the order readback screen.

The advanced order ticket works the same way, only it allows you to choose from more advanced strategies, such as selling short, all-or-none orders, and so on. *(Courtesy of Ameritrade)*

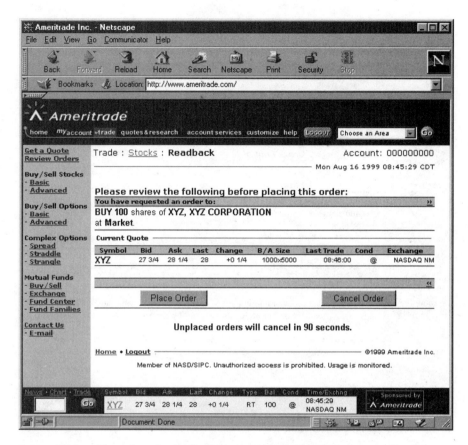

Figure 3-13. This is the order readback screen. Regardless of whether you used a market or limit order, or placed an option or mutual fund order, this screen always appears to give you the opportunity to confirm the order entered. In the example shown, it is an order to buy 100 shares of XYZ at market. A real-time quote also appears so that you have a better idea of the stock's current price.

If everything is correct with the order, you click the "place order" button, which will transmit the order to Ameritrade. If you decide not to place the order at this time, click the "cancel order" button. If you do nothing within 90 seconds, the order is canceled. *(Courtesy of Ameritrade)*

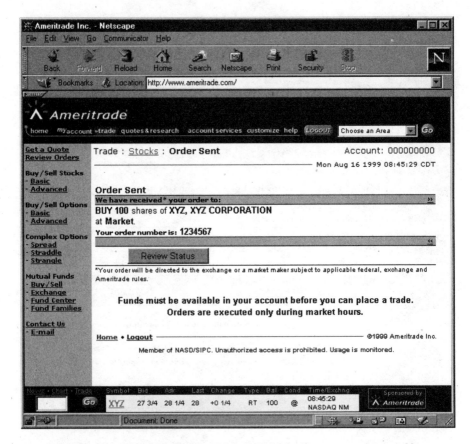

Figure 3-14. This screen is confirmation that the order has been sent and received by Ameritrade. An order number is given so that you can track this particular order. You can also at this point click the "review status" page, which will show whether or not your order has been executed. *(Courtesy of Ameritrade)*

Figure 3-15. This shows the home page for BuyandHold.com. Get started investing by taking advantage of what BuyandHold.com has to offer. *(Courtesy of BuyandHold.com)*

Figure 3-16. You can easily select stocks from its list of companies by browsing them by category, by alphabetical listing, or by searching. *(Courtesy of BuyandHold.com)*

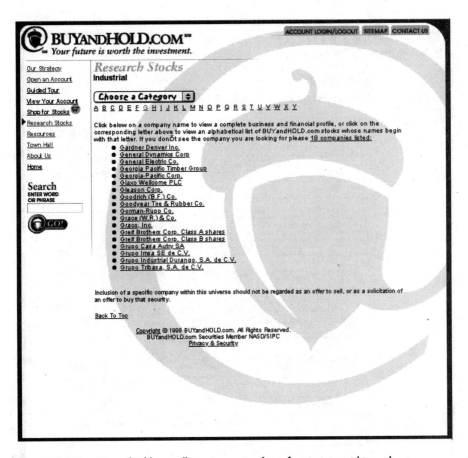

Figure 3-17. BuyandHold.com allows you to view lists of companies within each category, sorted alphabetically, so that you can easily find a company. *(Courtesy of BuyandHold.com)*

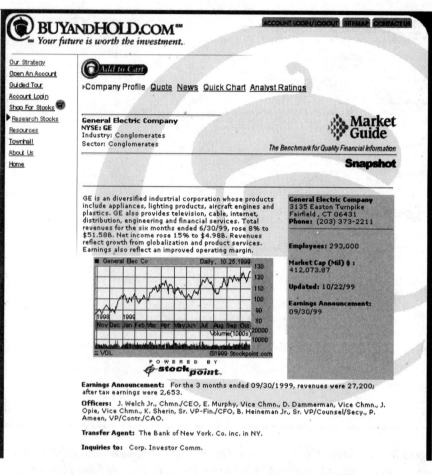

Figure 3-18. When you click on a company's name, you will be presented with a consolidated profile of the company. To purchase stock in this company, click "add to cart" and begin BuyandHold.com's unique Shop for Stocks℠ experience. *(Courtesy of BuyandHold.com)*

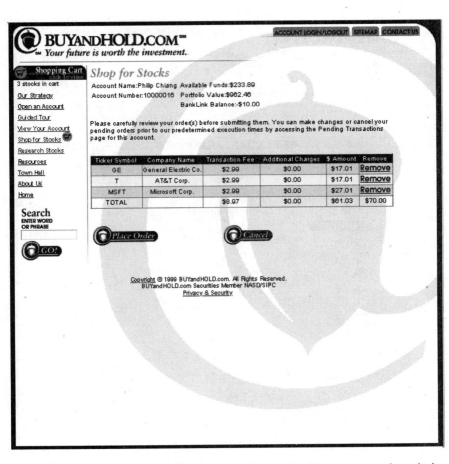

Figure 3-19. The shopping cart makes it easy to diversify by allowing you to make multiple purchases simultaneously. You can also review the stocks that you've added to your cart before making any purchases. *(Courtesy of BuyandHold.com)*

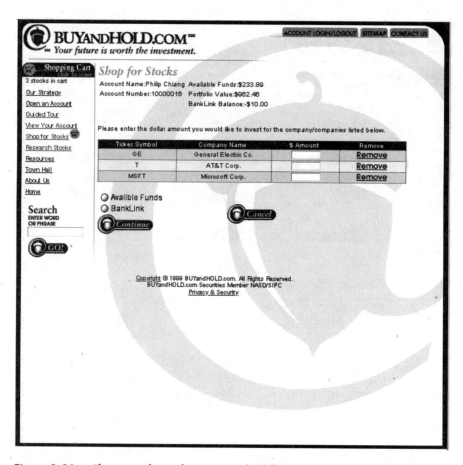

Figure 3-20. This screen shows where to enter the dollar amount to invest. Once the dollar amount is entered, BuyandHold.com will buy the appropriate number of shares, and then you proceed to checkout. *(Courtesy of BuyandHold.com)*

MAIN POINTS TO REMEMBER

- Manage the investments online that you are comfortable with; the majority of people have multiple accounts whether they are entirely online or split between both discount brokers and offline brokerage firms.

- Almost every type of investment can be made online, but the most common are stock transactions.

- Get all of your information ready before you sit down with the account papers so that you can expedite the process and begin trading in the timeliest manner possible.

4

CHOOSING THE BEST ONLINE BROKERAGE FIRM FOR YOU

DISCOUNT VS. FULL-PRICE BROKERS

Full-price brokers are what are commonly thought of as stock brokers or financial planners. For years, they have assisted investors in placing their trades, supplying them with information, and being their trusted "full-service" financial advisor. For their services, they receive a commission on every trade you place. The greatest asset brokers can give their customers is information. Until a few years ago, stock quotes, research, and other timely information were only available to these limited few, making the consumer an unwilling victim of "overpriced information." With the advent of the Internet, this information is everywhere, updated constantly, and mostly free. Although some people take comfort in the thought of a full-service broker who is always looking out for their best interest, in most cases this is simply not true. With so many clients and ever-dwindling margins on what they can charge to place a trade, full-price brokers are motivated more than ever to have as many clients as possible and make as many trades for these accounts as they can. The clients with the most money get the most attention; it is that simple. For those people who do not have a couple of hours a week or a desire to learn more about their investments, brokers provide a good escape. Some brokers do provide sound financial advice and help their clients in many ways; however, in this day and age it takes very little to receive the same information your broker gives you whenever you want it, and for free to boot. Although there are still thousands of full-price brokers, their days of reign are over. Even the investment banks are setting up online brokerage firms to compete directly with their full-price services. These banks realize that there is no way to stop the momentum of online investing, and it is only a matter of time before full-price brokers become an endangered species.

Discount brokers have actually been around for a long time, but they have begun appearing online only in the last couple of years. It is extremely difficult for traditional brokerage firms to go online because they have such high overhead from having to pay all of their brokers. The new wave of online investing firms employ fewer brokers and have so much of the process automated that they can afford to charge much lower commissions. In addition, the advent of the Internet allows them to provide a constantly updated wealth of information to their investors via their web site. Investors can access this information at any time and from any place with Internet access. Therefore, investors can place their trades at any time and from any place with Internet access as well. It is like having your own personal broker available whenever you desire.

WHAT MAKES THEM DIFFERENT?

Although discount brokers may not have the ability to provide you with the same level of personal attention as a full-service broker, they make up for it in many different ways. There are so many resources available online that all you have to do is spend a little time each week managing your account. Discount brokers are "discount" in the sense that they do not charge you as much. Financial information is provided to you via the computer instead of through a broker's mouth. In addition, you can place any size trade you like and pay between $3 and $30 instead of hundreds of dollars. Would you rather spend the money for so-called expert advice, or be able to buy an additional 20 to 30 shares of stock? Traditional brokers should be fearful of losing their jobs in that they are now giving advice from the same information that you yourself can access online. Discount brokers definitely do not provide the same level of "personal service" as traditional full-service brokers, but they give you the tools to maximize your investment capital in ways that have never been available to the individual investor.

GETTING COMFORTABLE WITH ONLINE INVESTING

Even if you are still feeling uncomfortable with online investing, there are certain ways to ease yourself into it. As we mentioned before, certain online brokerages, such as E*TRADE (www.etrade.com), offer a simulation game that allows you to invest with a pretend portfolio of $100,000. They even have cash prizes for the winners every month. Starting with "play money" will allow you to get comfortable with placing a trade online and using the services of an online broker. It will also get you in the habit of actively managing your account and getting familiar with web sites devoted to personal finance. There is so much information and so many online brokers on the Internet; the key is finding your niche and sticking to the web sites that are most suited to your personal investment strategy. There is something on the Internet for every level of online investor. This chapter examines the top online brokerage firms.

WHICH IS BEST FOR YOU?

There are over 100 online trading firms available on the Internet, and each one is different in its own way. Depending on your current level of investing and Internet usage, certain online brokers are going to make for a much better experience. The key is finding the ones that are best suited to your investment profile. Many online investors belong to more than one online broker in order to take advantage of certain opportunities available to their clients only, such as initial public offerings (IPOs). Other online brokerage firms are devoted to beginning investors and do not offer some of the more advanced features, such as the ability to trade options or futures. These brokers hold your hand through every step of a trade and often offer excellent customer service, with brokers ready to handle your questions at any time via the phone. The following pages explain the differences between the top online brokerage firms and the advantages for each level of investor.

There are certain key aspects to look for when selecting an online broker. Just because an online broker charges only $5 a trade does not mean that the broker is the best. In fact, the broker may be ill-equipped to handle customer service calls or may have frequent outages in its service. Other online brokers may offer special features, such as after-hours trading or the ability to trade your account by telephone as well as the Internet in case you cannot get to a computer. Selecting an online broker is actually the hardest part of online investing. You might start asking yourself, What makes online investing so different from everything I've done up until now? In many ways, they are exactly the same thing. Basically you find a stock you'd like to buy, you purchase it, you decide to keep it based on its performance, and you hope you make some money. Because there are so many choices, with so many different features, many people may not be aware of all the excellent benefits online brokerage firms offer. Some of these features will enhance your ability to manage your account and invest in alternative securities, while other features may just make your experience more confusing. Because each online brokerage firm caters to a specific level of investor, it is important to match your needs with those offered by the different firms.

Let's take a look at the different online brokerage firms and find the one that best fits your needs. It is a good idea to select a couple from these pages and then navigate around their web site to find the one you are most comfortable with.

OVERVIEW OF DIFFERENT ONLINE

AB WATLEY
www.abwatley.com

Overview: An overall good site for the more advanced trader, AB Watley's Watley Trader is an excellent application for people comfortable with technology. With electronic communication network (ECN) access and fully interactive charts, it is a great option for the more active trader. However, with no ability to get in on IPOs or access institutional research, you still need to add other web sites to your repertoire.

Advantages: ECN access, Nasdaq Level II quotes, interactive charting, weekend customer service, online chat rooms

Disadvantages: No access to IPOs or institutional research, lack of fundamental financial guidance

Most Suited For: Active traders

Minimum Balance: $3,000 for basic Watley Trader

Cost Per Stock Trade: As low as $9.95

Investments/Services Offered: Stocks, mutual funds, options, bonds

Other: Proprietary AB Watley trader software

AMERITRADE
www.ameritrade.com

Overview: Ameritrade continues to be one of the least expensive online brokers, but it lacks the customization features and advanced options needed to vault it to the top of the pack. Ameritrade is an excellent starting point for new online investors who are just interested in limited aspects of online investing; however, the lack of features make it difficult to capitalize on all of the opportunities offered by online investing.

Advantages: Inexpensive, electronic trade confirmation, ability to talk to a live broker when making the trade

Disadvantages: Lacks advanced functions, average customer service

Most Suited For: Beginners

Minimum Balance: $2,000 in cash or securities

Cost Per Stock Trade: As low as $8 per stock trade

Investments/Services Offered: Stocks, bonds, mutual funds, options, treasuries

Other: Options trading simulation game

BUYANDHOLD.COM
www.buyandhold.com

Overview: The focus and investment objective of BuyandHold.com is to cater to the needs of long-term investors following the principles of the buy-and-hold strategy. BuyandHold.com offers its customers the ability to buy and sell stocks for a fixed low commission and offers educational investment content, research, and planning aids from leading providers. The low minimum investment ($20) is manageable for most investors. This allows investors to maximize their investment dollar by providing an opportunity to spread their investment dollars over several selections while putting time and the effects of compounding on their side.

Advantages: Low minimum investment amount, diversification even at small dollar amount levels, financial planning tools

Disadvantages: Oriented to real beginners, delayed quotes

Most Suited For: Beginners and those with very limited capital; also a great gift idea for kids

Minimum Balance: $20

Cost Per Stock Trade: $2.99 for each transaction

Investments/Services Offered: Stocks

Other: Great new concept for beginning investors to get started or to educate children

CHARLES SCHWAB
www.schwab.com

Overview: Schwab continues to excel in the online broker-age ranks as it combines the features of online investing with actual investment broker professionals when needed. Although still one of the most expensive online brokerage firms, Schwab offers everything an online investor could need. Few can match its excellent research, planning, and customization tools. Look for its prices to decrease in the future.

Advantages: Customized home page, IPOs, bill paying, excellent 24/7 customer service, financial and tax planning tools, glossary

Disadvantages: Expensive (watch out for additional charges when making customer service phone calls)

Most Suited For: All levels

Minimum Balance: $1,000 for an IRA, $500 for a college account, or $5,000 for a normal brokerage account

Cost Per Stock Trade: As low as $29.95 per trade

Investments/Services Offered: Stocks, mutual funds, bonds, treasuries, options, CDs and money markets, annu-ities, life insurance

Other: Investment advisors for certain level accounts, mul-tilingual account representatives, enhanced research for active traders

DATEK
www.datek.com

Overview: Datek offers a full range of investment options. Its low price for trades makes it one of the most popular online brokerages; however, certain aspects of its web site are better suited for the more advanced and active traders. Look for Datek, with its proprietary interest in the Island ECN, to continue to specialize in services for more advanced investors.

Advantages: Express login screen, extended hours trading, special features for active investors and day traders

Disadvantages: Does not offer options, lacks extensive financial planning tools

Most Suited For: Intermediate to advanced

Minimum Balance: $2,000

Cost Per Stock Trade: As low as $9.99

Investments/Services Offered: Stocks, mutual funds

Other: Owner of Island Electronic Communication Network (ECN)

DLJDIRECT
www.dljdirect.com

Overview: DLJ combines the power of one of the most respected investment banking firms on Wall Street with its online investing arm DLJdirect. Although better suited to the more affluent investor, DLJdirect has many features and offers to its investors with $100,000 or more in assets access to the exclusive DLJ IPOs and equity research. An excellent online brokerage firm with many features for the online investor, DLJdirect is ideal for individuals who have been in the market for a while and are looking to make the switch to online investing.

Advantages: DLJ research and IPOs, same price to place trades by phone, 24/7 customer service, access to investment professionals, excellent stock price tracking

Disadvantages: Expensive commissions, $100,000 in assets required to take advantage of IPOs and equity research

Most Suited For: Advanced investors

Minimum Balance: No minimum balance

Cost Per Stock Trade: Flat fee of $20 per trade up to 1,000 shares for stocks

Investments/Services Offered: Stocks, mutual funds, treasuries, municipals, governments, precious metals, bonds, options, IPOs

E*TRADE

www.etrade.com

Overview: E*TRADE is rated by many as the number one online broker. Probably the most well known, E*TRADE has continuously upgraded its services in order to provide a better experience for its investors. E*TRADE also offers a host of other services including accounting and financial planning tools, message boards, IPOs, banking, and institutional research. E*TRADE will also soon be offering after-hours trading for more advanced investors via Instinet (Power E*TRADE).

Advantages: Offers a comprehensive set of tools for both beginning and advanced online investors, including the

E*TRADE games that allow you to invest online with a practice portfolio

Disadvantages: Lacks extensive tools for an investor interested in one specific area of online investing

Most Suited For: Beginning to advanced investors who have a general interest in online investing

Minimum Balance: Free membership for basic tools, $1,000 to open a normal account

Cost Per Stock Trade: As low as $14.95

Investments/Services Offered: Stocks, options, IPOs, bonds, mutual funds, banking, retirement, mortgages, insurance, taxes

Other: Often runs promotions of cash or reward points to open an account.

FIDELITY
www.fidelity.com

Overview: Fidelity has slowly but surely made its way into the upper echelons of online investing firms. Always having a wealth of resources for investors, including financial and tax planning tools, Fidelity has added to its arsenal after-hours trading, wireless trading, and IPO opportunities. Look for Fidelity to continue to offer excellent new features for online investors.

Advantages: Wireless trading, excellent research, broad range of investment opportunities, active trading options

Disadvantages: High commissions for most securities

Most Suited For: Both beginner and advanced traders

Minimum Balance: $2,500

Cost Per Stock Trade: As low as $14.95

Investments/Services Offered: Stocks, bonds, IPOs, mutual funds, annuities, life insurance

Other: Bill paying

FIRSTRADE
www.firstrade.com

Overview: A great place for beginners to start, Firstrade combines excellent customer support with an easy-to-use graphic interface and some of the lowest fees around. In addition, you can speak with a registered broker to place a trade (although it costs a bit more) or place it over your telephone. Although Firstrade lacks some of the more extensive financial and tax planning tools, it is an excellent place for new online investors.

Advantages: Customer service, low fees, easy to use

Disadvantages: Lack of financial planning tools

Most Suited For: Beginners

Minimum Balance: No minimum balance

Cost Per Stock Trade: As low as $6.95

Investments/Services Offered: Stocks, mutual funds, options

Other: Extensive section on frequently asked questions

MORGAN STANLEY DEAN WITTER ONLINE
www.online.msdw.com or *www.discoverbrokerage.com*

Overview: Morgan Stanley Dean Witter Online, formerly Discover brokerage, continues to be an extremely efficient and reliable online broker. Having recently introduced after-hours trading, it is beginning to offer additional features to more advanced online investors. Although only investors with $100,000 in assets can take advantage of the Morgan Stanley IPOs, there is a wealth of other resources that make this a top online brokerage firm.

Advantages: After-hours trading, 24/7 customer service, Morgan Stanley research and IPOs, trade stocks on the Palm III

Disadvantages: IPOs only available to investors with more than $100,000 on account

Most Suited For: Advanced investors

Minimum Balance: $2,000 in cash or stock

Cost Per Stock Trade: As low as $14.95 for stock trades

Investments/Services Offered: Stocks, mutual funds, bonds, treasuries, options

Other: Customer service with a registered representative, on the Internet or over the phone

MURIEL SIEBERT & CO.
www.msiebert.com

Overview: Siebert offers a wide range of products and services for beginner and advanced investors alike. Offering everything from IPOs to services for active traders, Siebert combines an easy-to-use interface with excellent features for the online investor. In addition, investors receive the monthly newsletter from Muriel Siebert, renowned market analyst.

Advantages: Broad services, IPOs, active trader options

Disadvantages: Real-time updates

Most Suited For: Intermediates

Minimum Balance: No minimum balance

Cost Per Stock Trade: As low as $14.95 for stock transactions

Investments/Services Offered: Stocks, bonds, mutual funds, options

Other: Limited regional offices

NATIONAL DISCOUNT BROKERS (NDB)
www.ndb.com

Overview: One of the biggest online brokerages, NDB has a wide range of investment services and offers some of the best educational content on online investing. NDB lacks a bit in planning tools, but it is an excellent first step for new online investors. It has an easy-to-use web site and great educational content for new online investors.

Advantages: Educational content, news alerts, ease of use

Disadvantages: No access to IPOs or research

Most Suited For: Beginners to advanced

Minimum Balance: No minimum balance

Cost Per Stock Trade: As low as $14.75 for market order over the Internet

Investments/Services Offered: Stocks, mutual funds, bonds, options

Other: Place trades over the phone or with the online broker

PEREMEL

www.peremel.com

Overview: Peremel offers two different account structures: one oriented toward an individual still interested in dealing with a broker, and another strictly for online trading. This two-tier system has its advantages for online investors who just aren't ready to let go of having the guidance of a broker.

Advantages: Web site design, research, customer service

Disadvantages: Account information

Most Suited For: Beginners to intermediates

Minimum Balance: $2,000

Cost Per Stock Trade: $35 plus $.03 per share using a broker, or $18 for a trade strictly online

Investments/Services Offered: Stocks, mutual funds, IPOs, options

Other: Account demo available online

QUICK & REILLY
www.quick-reilly.com

Overview: Quick & Reilly offers two different ways to invest in order to cater to the beginner and more advanced online investor. Its web site is a bit outdated, but it provides excellent round-the-clock customer service and competitive fees. In addition, the site also has extensive research information and charting capabilities in order to monitor your stocks.

Advantages: Round-the-clock customer service, researching capabilities, caters to different level investors, access to licensed brokers

Disadvantages: Outdated web site

Most Suited For: Beginners and intermediates

Minimum Balance: No minimum balance

Cost Per Stock Trade: As low as $37.50

Investments/Services Offered: Stocks, mutual bonds, CDs, options

Other: 120 offices nationwide

SURETRADE
www.suretrade.com

Overview: Suretrade has a very easy-to-use site that is excellent for new online investors. With extremely low commissions and features such as a glossary and free research, Suretrade is an excellent place to get your feet wet with online investing. Although the customer service can be a bit slow at times, the web site is extremely straightforward and easy to navigate.

Advantages: Low commissions, glossary, easy-to-use web site

Disadvantages: Slow customer service, lacks features for advanced or active investors

Most Suited For: Beginners

Minimum Balance: No minimum balance

Cost Per Stock Trade: As low as $7.95 for stocks

Investments/Services Offered: Stocks, mutual funds, bonds, treasuries, options

---

TD WATERHOUSE
www.tdwaterhouse.com

Overview: TD Waterhouse is the combination of Toronto Dominion Bank and Waterhouse Securities. An excellent overall web site, an extensive investor learning area makes TD Waterhouse one of the best online brokers for beginning investors. TD Waterhouse also has one of the best customer service centers to help with all of your queries.

Advantages: Easy-to-use web site, customer service

Disadvantages: Lacks advanced investor tools

Most Suited For: Beginners

Minimum Balance: $1,000

Cost Per Stock Trade: As low as $12

Investments/Services Offered: Stocks, mutual funds, bonds, CDs, unit investment trusts (UITs), options

Other: Online trading demo

THE NET INVESTOR
www.netinvestor.com

Overview: The Net Investor is most suited for investors who are intermediate to advanced in their understanding of investments. The Net Investor does not offer much for the beginning investor, but it does have real-time quotes, charts, research, fast execution, and excellent customer service.

Advantages: Customer service, real-time quotes

Disadvantages: Educational information, expensive, poor site design

Most Suited For: Intermediate to advanced investors

Minimum Balance: No minimum balance

Cost Per Stock Trade: $19.95 plus $.01 per share for stock trades

Investments/Services Offered: Stocks, mutual funds, bonds, options, IPOs, CDs

Other: A division of Howe Barnes Investments

TRADESCAPE.COM
www.tradescape.com

Overview: Tradescape.com has recently entered the online brokerage scene and caters to active traders and mostly day traders. With its proprietary interest in Tradescape 1.0, this site allows active traders to trade directly through electronic communications networks (ECNs). Look for its technology to become mainstream very soon. This is not a service for those new to online trading.

Advantages: Access to Level II quotes, trade directly/cut out the broker, Tradescape 1.0 software

Disadvantages: Active traders only

Most Suited For: Active traders

Minimum Balance: No minimum balance

Cost Per Stock Trade: As low as $1.50 for 100 shares, plus a monthly charge of $79.99 for direct access to the markets

Investments/Services Offered: Stocks

Other: First firm to offer the ability to skip the broker altogether and access the markets directly from the Internet

---

WANG

www.wangvest.com

Overview: Wang Investments provides strong services to the more advanced investor. Although it does not provide as much guidance as many other sites, it has excellent execution and inexpensive fees that make it very attractive. In addition, there is a Chinese version of the site.

Advantages: Inexpensive fees, range of investment tools

Disadvantages: Lack of investment guidance

Most Suited For: Intermediate to advanced investors

Minimum Balance: No minimum balance, a $20 fee is charged if less than $5,000

Cost Per Stock Trade: As low as $8 for stocks

Investments/Services Offered: Stocks, bonds, mutual funds, options, CDs

Other: Additional Chinese version of site

WIT CAPITAL
www.witcapital.com

Overview: Wit Capital is currently the top place on the web for online investors to get in on IPOs. Its lack of extensive financial planning tools makes this an excellent "second account" to take advantage of the investment banking activities. Look for a new site design and added features that will make this a more user-friendly site for beginner online investors.

Advantages: Leading IPO online broker, good institutional research, private placement opportunities

Disadvantages: Lacks basic financial tools for investors, selling an IPO too fast will make it difficult to get in on future IPOs offered by them

Most Suited For: Investors with an interest in IPOs and private equity deals

Minimum Balance: $2,000

Cost Per Stock Trade: As low as $14.95

Investments/Services Offered: Stocks, options, bonds, mutual funds, IPOs, private placements

Other: Email alerts of IPO opportunities

BROKERAGE FIRMS

OTHER ONLINE INVESTING FIRMS

Accutrade	www.accutrade.com
American Century	www.americancentury.com

American Express Direct	www.americanexpress.com/direct
Bank of America Investment Services, Inc.	www.bankofamerica.com/ investments
Bank One	www.oneinvest.com
BCL	www.bclnet.com
Bidwell	www.bidwell.com
Brown	www.brownco.com
Bull & Bear	www.bullbear.com
Citicorp Investments	www.citibank.com
Computel	www.computel.com
Dreyfus	www.dreyfus.com
Empire	www.empirenow.com
FBR.com	www.fbr.com
Freeman Welwood	www.freemanwelwood.com
InvesTrade	www.investrade.com
JB Oxford	www.jboxford.com
Mr. Stock	www.mrstock.com
My Discount Broker	www.mydiscountbroker.com
Regal Securities	www.eregal.com
Scottrade	www.scottrade.com
Trading Direct	www.tradingdirect.com
UMC	www.umcstock.com
US Rica Financial	www.usrica.com
Vision Trade	www.visiontrade.com
WallStreet Electronica	www.wallstreete.com
Web Street	www.webstreet.com
WellsTrade	www.wellsfargo.com/wellstrade
Wingspan	www.wingspan.com
Worldtrade	www.worldtradefinancial.com

Wyse   www.wyse-sec.com

MAIN POINTS TO REMEMBER

- Each online broker offers different features for specific level investors.
- Just because an online broker has the cheapest prices per transaction does not mean it is the best online broker.
- Select three or four online brokers that sound like they match your needs and navigate through their web sites to get a feeling about the best one for you.

C H A P T E R

5

INVESTMENT OPTIONS

WHAT INVESTMENTS SHOULD YOU MANAGE ONLINE?

Every one of your investments can be managed online. Some are easier to manage online than others, depending on your comfort level with the Internet and the nature of your investments. For example, putting a standard monthly amount into your IRA in a mutual fund can be done much easier over the Internet than by talking by phone with your broker. If you are looking to invest in tax-free municipal bonds, however, it may make more sense to consult your broker about which bonds would be the most advantageous for your current tax situation (although there is plenty of information online about tax-free municipal bonds if you have the desire to research it). Almost 90 percent of what everyone invests in are fairly straightforward investments in stocks or mutual funds. The tools to research them and make transactions are not only available online but are so easy to use and affordable that brokers are truly not needed for these sorts of investments.

Investors have different goals for their investments. Some hold stocks a lifetime, whereas others make intra-day trades. Different online brokerages are better for each type of investor. Everyone can take advantage of online investing in order to purchase almost every stock and mutual fund imaginable. Take a look at your investments. What are your goals for each of these investments? Are there particular investments that you make repeatedly over the course of the year? Are you an active or passive investor? These are the sorts of questions that will help you determine which investments to manage online.

Each online investor takes advantage of the functionality of online investing for a different reason. Some people look to transfer the bulk of their investments to their online brokerage account. Others look to start from scratch with new investments. There are investors who place some trades online and some with a broker. Other investors invest only online. Some online investors look to take part in IPOs only, whereas others like the access to make or research their trade at any time of day. The key point is that you can tailor online investing to whatever level is in your best interest and manage your investments online. And remember, by opening an online brokerage account, you will pay much less in commissions for a trade, and maybe you'll save enough in commissions to buy an extra share or two of stock.

Purchasing a stock online is extremely easy. (At the end of this chapter we take you step by step through placing a trade with three different online brokers.) With online investing there is no more waiting for your broker to call back and inform you if your trade was confirmed; in most cases you will receive your confirmation electronically in a matter of seconds. In addition, you can monitor your portfolio at any time, day or night, and have access to breaking news and research. Buying a stock online has exactly the same outcome as if you had asked your broker to buy a stock. By eliminating the middleman (the broker), you save yourself time and money. You now have access to virtually the same information as your broker, and the ability to make more informed investment decisions—with your own best interests in mind at all times.

So how you do you know which investments you should manage online? Whatever you are comfortable with. Becoming accustomed to online investing, like anything else, takes time. Start off making simple stock trades, or practice with a mock portfolio and learn how to take advantage of the various capabilities of online investing. Once you are comfortable making simple trades, consider the numerous other opportunities such as bonds, options, and CDs that you can invest in online as well.

Whether you are saving for college, a house, kids, a car, or a comfortable retirement, online investing is an empowering tool that will make managing your investments easier and save you money.

WHAT INVESTMENTS CAN YOU PURCHASE ONLINE?

The most popular online investment is stocks. Whether buying an individual stock, investing in a mutual fund, or taking part in IPOs, the bulk of trades placed online is for stocks. The key is to get comfortable with stocks first and then examine moving on to more advanced investment options.

Although each online broker is set up a little differently, placing a trade is fundamentally the same. Yet there are a number of ways that you can customize your particular trade. For example, you can set a stop/loss order, which means that your stock will automatically be sold if it drops to a certain level. You can short a stock in hopes that the stock price will drop. Later in this chapter we explain what

each of these terms means and your full range of options when placing a trade. For anyone just starting out, purchasing stocks online is
the easiest way to get your feet wet in online investing. Each online
broker offers different features and various advanced investment
options; however, most offer all of the publicly traded stocks on the
U.S. equity markets.

Stocks. Investing in the right mix of stocks has produced over time
some of the best returns for the individual investor. The key is obvi-
ously knowing which stocks to invest in and at what point. Fortunately, online investing puts all of the information you need right at
your fingertips. As we discuss in Chapter 8, the amazing number of
web sites devoted to the individual investor can present you with an
unprecedented amount of information to use when making your
investment decisions. The Internet makes researching and investing
in stocks easier than it has ever been before. Although certain stocks
may be in the spotlight today, the savvy investor is always on the
lookout for great stocks in the future. There are now more choices
than ever of public stocks that you can invest in. For a long time many
conservative individuals looked to blue chip stocks on the New York
Stock Exchange (NYSE) and tried to avoid the smaller stocks on the
American Stock Exchange (Amex) or the National Association of
Securities Dealers (Nasdaq). Stocks traded on the NYSE, also called
the "Big Board," were for a long time the most heavily traded stocks
and on average gradually produced above average returns for their
investors. Technology stocks are now the mostly heavily traded
stocks and are mostly listed on the Nasdaq. The rise of the technology
sector, specifically the Internet, has dramatically increased the overall
volume of shares being traded and has vaulted the Nasdaq into the
spotlight as a result. There is no denying that stocks, and the market
as a whole, change over time as we have seen with the emergence of
the Nasdaq. As an online investor, it does not make much difference
which exchange the stocks you trade are on. You are still able to buy
and sell in the exact same manner and from any online brokerage

firm. The rise of technology stocks simply gives you more exciting places to invest your money.

All stocks are susceptible to different amounts of market and industry risk. There are times when the market as a whole is very bullish or bearish and can force a stock up or down because of general market sentiment. Other times a particular industry can be in or out of favor, driving the prices of stocks within that industry in a certain direction. There are so many stocks to choose from that you can tailor your portfolio to meet your risk/reward profiles. Online investing gives you the opportunity to invest in as many shares of any stock you choose. There is no more having to place an order for 100 shares with your broker in order to make a trade, you can buy as little as one share of a stock and build your holdings over time. You can even buy fractions of shares of stock over time through certain online brokers. There are also certain stocks that you can now buy directly from the company. Stocks within certain industries are prone to more fluctuation over time. Technology stocks certainly fall into this category because the industry is changing so rapidly. However, every stock goes up and down over time and those that move the most give you the best opportunity to make a significant amount of money over time.

Mutual funds. Traditionally considered one of the best places to start investing, mutual funds, which are most often managed by a seasoned money manager, are appealing to individuals because they perform almost like a miniportfolio. There are almost 10,000 different mutual fund options available to the individual investor. Many funds are part of families, which means there are a variety of different funds managed by the same group, such as Janus or Vanguard. Most of these fund families have their own web sites. These web sites provide information about an individual fund's goals, historical performance, and fees, all of which can be found in the prospectus.

The Internet can help you to find the best funds in each class. Some of the best sites for comparative research are Morningstar (www.morningstar.com), Business Week (www.businessweek.com),

Barron's (www.barrons.com), and Forbes (www.forbes.com). You do not have to buy your mutual fund online through your broker; you can buy directly from the company online. You can choose to make a one-time purchase of a mutual fund, which usually requires a minimum investment, or you can opt for its automatic investment plan. Enrollment in these plans often waives or reduces the initial fee. Here are just a few of the places you can purchase the fund directly. For more sites, perform a search on a search engine such as Excite (www.excite.com) or a directory such as Yahoo (www.yahoo.com).

Dreyfus Funds (www.dreyfus.com)

Evergreen Funds (www.evergreen.com)

Janus Funds (www.janus.com)

John Hancock Funds (www.jhancock.com)

Merrill Lynch Funds (www.plan.ml.com/products-services)

Prudential Funds (www.prudential.com)

Scudder Funds (www.scudder.com)

Smith Barney Funds (www.smithbarney.com)

Of course, you also have the option of buying mutual funds from an online broker. A complete list and analysis of online brokers is in Chapter 4.

Initial public offerings. There has been a lot of attention surrounding initial public offerings (IPOs) lately due to the amazing rise of numerous technology stocks. Some Internet stocks have even doubled or tripled in value on their first day of trading. Although this is not always the case, many investors for the first time have been able to participate in these IPOs through underwriters that have reserved shares for online investors. Companies such as Wit Capital (www.witcapital.com) and E*Offering (www.eoffering.com) specifically focus on offering shares of IPOs to online investors. Other web sites such as IPO.com (www.ipo.com) offer tons of information on upcoming IPOs. Shares of stock in IPOs used to be reserved for a brokerage firm's best spending clients. With the rise of the Internet and online investing, these shares are now being shared with the public, giving you the chance to get in on the ground floor.

When a company goes public, it is required to file an S-1 with the SEC and release a prospectus to current investors. The prospectus is like the business plan for the company and is your best source of information to learn about the business. It contains information on the company's future plans, risks, competition, and financial situation. You can get a copy of the prospectus by contacting the company directly or by going to a web site such as www.ipo.com to have it sent to you. Most people do not take the time to read the prospectus carefully. They should because between the limited legal jargon are pages of excellent information on the future direction of the business.

It is important to realize that even with the latest results of companies going public, there are often times when a company's IPO can be a flop. As with any stock, there is no set formula as to whether the stock goes up or down on its first day of trading. When a company has an IPO, the first day of trading is largely based on momentum and determined by the large institutions buying the biggest blocks of shares. The best way to get an idea for how these institutions will be reacting is to find research on what the Wall Street analysts are saying about the stock. This information can be found by actually purchasing the reports from The Investext Group (www.investext.com) or Thomson Investor Network (www.thomsoninvest.com), or by obtaining a concise free version at Zacks Investment Research (www.zacks.com). It is important to note that analysts cannot release their first "official" research report on a company until the stock has been trading for a specific number of days. In addition, before a company goes public, it is forced to enter a "quiet period." Therefore, finding information on companies that have a scheduled IPO can be a bit difficult. The most obvious ways to get information are to request a prospectus or look at the S-1 document (registration papers) filed with the SEC when the company announced its intention to sell shares to the public.

IPOs are an excellent way to diversify the mix of your portfolio. Although IPOs are a more aggressive investment, investors that have gotten in on the ground floor have achieved some of the highest returning investments of all time. However, do not purchase shares expecting the value to double on the first day of trading. Even though numerous technology stocks have done this, all but a handful have settled down after their first few days of trading. The most important aspect is to select stocks you think are valuable businesses. These are the stocks that will gradually appreciate over time and provide you with the best investment for your money.

A sample of IPO big winners and losers

Company	Opening Price	End-of-Quarter Price*
Internet Capital Group	$12	$87.88
Red Hat, Inc.	$14	$96
Alteon WebSystems	$19	$94
Net2Phone	$15	$52.13
Ketro Corporation	$8	$27.38
Kana Communications, Inc.	$15	$49.88
Quest Software, Inc.	$14	$46.50
Hotjobs.com, Ltd	$8	$25.38
China.com Corporation	$20	$65
Foundry Networks	$25	$126
MCM Capital Group, Inc.	$10	$4.75
JFAX.COM, Inc.	$9.50	$4.97
Cyber Merchants Exchange, Inc.	$8	$4.25
ProVantage Health Services, Inc.	$18	$10.31
Quokka Sports, Inc.	$12	$6.94
Voyager.net, Inc.	$15	$8.75
Continuus Software Corporation	$8	$4.75
The Keith Companies, Inc.	$9	$5.50
Webstakes.com, Inc.	$14	$8.88
Quotesmith.com, Inc.	$11	$7.13

*As of 10/31/99

Automatic monthly investment plans. Automatic monthly investment plans are one of the best ways to get into the habit of investing.
By setting up a direct deposit link with your online broker and your
bank, your online brokerage firm can automatically deduct a certain
amount each month and invest the funds in an investment such as a
mutual fund. Getting in the habit is never easy except when it happens all by itself. Automatic monthly investment plans are also great
for making contributions to your IRA. Most mutual fund companies
can set up an account with an initial deposit of $1,000 or $2,000.

Automatic monthly investment plans are a fantastic way to take
advantage of compounded interest. The following chart shows the
effects of saving a specific amount every month with the money
compounding annually starting in 1999.

	2000	2005	2010	2020	2035
Investor A ($100 a month)	$1,320	$10,185	$24,461	$84,483	$394,847
Investor B ($200 a month)	$2,640	$20,369	$48,922	$168,967	$789,695
Investor C ($500 a month)	$6,600	$50,923	$122,306	$422,416	$1,974,237
Investor D ($1,000 a month)	$13,200	$101,846	$244,611	$844,833	$3,948,474

The key is to start saving on a routine basis immediately.
Although there is never a guarantee that your money will grow at a
specific percentage year after year, the market has returned overall
positive returns over substantial periods of time. Regardless of
whether you have just started college or just entered your retirement,
it is never too late or too early to capitalize on the effects of compounded interest. In fact, if you had invested just $1,000 in AOL in
the beginning of 1998, it would have been worth approximately
$118,400 as of November 1999. This is an extreme case; however,
investing in the stock market is really about the appreciation of companies over time. The best way to capitalize on them is to invest rou-

tinely. Online investing and automatic monthly investment plans make it just that much easier.

Direct public offerings. A direct public offering (DPO) is a way for a company to offer shares directly to the public rather than offer them through a broker. It is essentially like filing for an IPO without the underwriter (investment banking firm). Since 1995, the general public has been able to receive a company's prospectus online. As you can imagine, the Internet has become an unprecedented resource for both companies seeking money to grow and investors vying for the opportunity to invest on the ground floor of a new company. The company saves by not having to pay the underwriter a huge fee and by using the Internet to cut down on distribution costs. Although DPOs are not nearly as popular as IPOs, they have been gaining popularity over the last couple of years. DPOs are certainly not short on appeal and excitement, but they should be entered into by only the most seasoned investor because these investments are high risk. Although they offer potentially huge rewards, you could wake to find your investment worth very little a day or a week after you have invested. DPOs are regulated by the SEC; however, it is still very important to do your homework before investing. You can get shares of a DPO through a subscription agreement form, usually the last page of the prospectus. Fill out this form completely and return it with your money to the company, who will then send you both a confirmation letter and a stock certificate. A great resource for information about and access to DPOs is Netstock Direct (www.netstockdirect.com).

Direct purchase plans. Over the past few years, many public companies have started offering their shares directly to the public through programs referred to as direct purchase plans. DPPs (sometimes called no-load stock plans) allow individuals to buy stock directly from the company without having to first buy stock through a broker. Whereas some DPPs allow only large companies to partic-ipate in their plans, many are available to individuals as well. These companies include Ford, IBM, Wal-Mart, and many others. The number of companies that offer DPPs is now over 1,000, and the number of individuals currently taking advantage of these programs tops 1 million. These plans also have many dividend reinvestment features.

Investing in a DPP can be a wise investment decision for those who do not have much money to start investing (you can start with some companies for less than $50). Contact can be made in most cases either by phone or mail, or online to the company's Investor Relations department. The company will tell you whether it offers a DPP and will send you information and an application. Simply return the completed application and a check to the company (remembering to make copies for your records) via registered mail. Many DPPs require as little as $300 to start, and purchases after the initial one can often be under $20.

Keep in mind that investing with DPPs is not designed for the active trader; trades can take up to a week. DPPs should be viewed as part of a person's long-term investing strategy. And while hassle free in some respects, DPPs also carry their own fees. Initial enroll-ment can cost anywhere from $5 to $15, and there are often other transaction and maintenance fees that are charged. As regulations continue to open doors for these plans, they will become both more convenient (buy your shares via the Internet) and competitive (rates will decrease as they compete against one another).

Dividend reinvestment plans. Dividend reinvestment plans (DRIPs), sometimes referred to as SIPs (Shareholder Investment Programs), offer investors an inexpensive way to buy stock and re-invest the dividend dollars to accumulate even more stock. DRIPs are offered by both large companies and mutual funds. Shares must be in your name, and after the first purchase, those shares bought directly from the company are often discounted between 3 and 5 percent (not to mention free of broker commissions). Most companies also allow options cash payments (OCPs) after the initial dividend reinvestment. These payments can be even less than $20, allowing investors to buy fractions of shares. Companies that offer DRIPs may vary in what they allow. Most have different rules with regard to reinvestment of dividends, the amount allowed for reinvestment, and OCPs. Also a great place to start for young investors, many DRIPs allow you to open a plan in someone else's name and help a young person understand one company and the investing process before tackling more advanced approaches—a great gift for a child.

Over 1,000 companies offer DRIPs. A complete list of companies offering DRIPs can be found at InvestorGuide (www.investorguide .com). Contacting the Investor Relations department of a public company is your best bet for getting information on that company's program.

ADDITIONAL INVESTMENT OPTIONS

Although we do not cover more advanced investments such as options, futures, or bonds in this book, there is a plethora of other investment options available for online investors. For example, if you have an account with Wit Capital (www.witcapital.com), you have access to the normal stocks and IPOs in addition to private equity deals (if you are an accredited investor). If you have an account at Ameritrade (www.ameritrade.com), you are also able to invest in bonds, CDs, and treasury bills.

It is important to recognize that buying and selling stocks online is just the tip of the iceberg for online investors. After you are comfortable with stocks, consider the wealth of other investment options, if you so desire. (A description of the investment options of leading brokerage firms is provided in Chapter 4.) Although a lot of people do take advantage of these other options, many online investors are content just to stick with buying and selling stocks.

Different industry sectors. There are approximately 28 different industry sectors, including over 300 different industries, comprising thousands of publicly trade companies. An industry is a segment of the business world; a sector is a particular group of stocks found within an industry. Although this may sound overwhelming, it is very easy to sort through the different stocks within these industries and find the ones that best fit your investment profile. At the end of this chapter are examples of specific stocks within these sectors; the Internet and online service providers, Internet and online content providers, and Internet and Intranet software and services. In addition, web sites such as Hoover's (www.hoovers.com) break down the different stocks by sector and industry and then provide their own overview and financial snapshot of each company. Reviewing this information is one of the best ways to begin looking for stocks to build your portfolio.

Perhaps the most well known industry today is technology, which has produced unprecedented returns for online investors over the last couple of years. Other industries such as consumer products and banking have been less glamorous but have produced steady returns for their investors over the last decade. Although each industry has its own historical patterns, there is no way to tell what an industry's stocks will do in the future. It is always a good idea to have a mix of stocks within different industries in your portfolio to protect yourself against a dip in any specific industry.

Just because technology stocks are prone to more risk does not mean that you should not take advantage of them for some part of your portfolio. Even within technology stocks there are certain ones that are prone to much more market risk than others. Companies such as Microsoft and Cisco have market capitalizations that are now among the biggest in the world. Investors who had the foresight a number of years ago to recognize the technology industry coming into favor have been rewarded handsomely for their efforts. In fact, millions of people are still capitalizing on the amazing rise of technology stocks such as Yahoo! and Amazon.com. Being able to recognize an industry coming into or going out of favor is a valuable skill that you learn only by managing your account and studying the markets.

Despite the fact that many people have been predicting the impending downturn of stocks over the last two years, more money than ever has been made during this period. There will always be naysayers in the market and people telling you to wait to invest; however, historic returns have shown there is no time like the present to begin investing your money. Investing in the right combination of stocks over time will yield above average returns even with downturns in the market. While waiting to invest, you are losing interest on your money that offsets most downturns over time. Keep your goals in mind. If you're planning for the long term, a temporary dip in the market will not hurt you as much as if you were to invest money needed in the next one or two years in a more volatile stock.

Each online investor has a different investment profile, which means he or she will invest in a different variety of industries. Make sure to spend some time familiarizing yourself with the variety of stocks within different industries. Online investing presents an amazing amount of information in an easy-to-understand format so that you can make your own investment decisions. All the information is out there; it is up to you to take advantage of it.

Industry sectors (Courtesy of Hoover's Online, www.hoovers.com)

Aerospace and Defense

Automotive and Transport Equipment

Banking

Chemicals

Computer Hardware

Computer Software and Services

Conglomerates

Consumer Products—Durables

Consumer Products—Nondurables

Diversified Services

Drugs

Electronics and Miscellaneous Technology

Energy

Financial Services

Food, Beverage, and Tobacco

Health Products and Services

Insurance

Leisure

Manufacturing

Materials and Construction

Media

Metals and Mining

Real Estate

Retail

Specialty Retail

Telecommunications

Transportation

Utilities

Stocks in the spotlight. Whether a certain industry is booming or a stock has produced amazing returns for its investors, certain stocks tend to be in the spotlight a lot more than others. Because they are in the spotlight, there are bound to be many more people trading the stock, creating a more volatile stock price. Remember, however, that just because a stock is in the spotlight today does not guarantee it will not fall out of favor tomorrow.

As of late, Internet and technology stocks specifically have received a lot of attention for their wild price swings. Even on a normal day, many Internet and technology stocks often move several points. For most stocks, a couple points of movement could take a week or even a month to achieve. Stocks such as Priceline.com, which debuted its IPO in 1999 and at the time was simply a bidding service for airline tickets, had a market capitalization greater than American Airlines within the first week.

It is amazing to note the dramatic rise of Internet and technology stocks in the marketplace. Never has so much wealth been generated in so little time. This is not to say that everyone has made money on these stocks. As with any volatile stock, there are downswings as well as upswings. However, there is no denying the incredible opportunities that you can capitalize on by having your money in stocks in the spotlight. Online investing allows you to very easily target these stocks and research ones that may become the next high flyer. For so many years, Wall Street pros were the only ones capitalizing on stocks in the spotlight because it took so much time for the word to get out to everyone else beyond the privileged few. The Internet has changed this, and now the information is available to everyone. One of the best ways to recognize a stock in the spotlight is just by looking at the volume of shares traded for the day compared to its historical volume levels. Almost all charts that show price will also give you volume levels. Web sites such as BigCharts (www.bigcharts.com) will give you everything you need. Remember, though, that the best time to buy these stocks is before everyone knows about them. Therefore, a little research is your best bet to identify these stocks before they have hit their high point. It is never a good idea to have too much of your portfolio locked up in these stocks; however, a good portion of your aggressive mix gives you the opportunity to maximize your investment capital over time.

STOCKS IN THE SPOTLIGHT

Internet and online service providers (Courtesy of Hoover's Online, www.hoovers.com)

Company Name	Ticker Symbol	Web Site
Allied Riser Communications Corporation	ARCC	www.alliedriser.com
AppliedTheory Corporation	ATHY	www.appliedtheory.com
BiznesOnline.com, Inc.	BIZZ	www.biznessonline.com
CAIS Internet, Inc.	CAIS	www.cais.com
Cavion Technologies, Inc.	CAVN	www.cavion.com
CommTouch Software Ltd.	CTCH	www.commtouch.com
Concentric Network Corporation	CNCX	www.concentric.com
Covad Communications Group, Inc.	COVD	www.covad.com
Digex, Incorporated	DIGX	www.digex.com
Digital Island, Inc.	ISLD	www.digisle.com
DSL.net, Inc.	DSLN	www.dsl.net
Earthlink Network, Inc.	ELNK	www.earthlink.net
EQUANT N.V.	ENT	www.equant.com
Euroweb International Corp.	EWEB	www.euroweb.hu
Excite@Home	ATHM	www.home.net
FlashNet Communications, Inc.	FLAS	www.flash.net
Freeserve plc	FREE	www.freeserve.net
Frontline Communications Corporation	FCCN	www.frontline.net
Globix Corporation	GBIX	www.globix.com
High Speed Access Corp.	HSAC	www.hsacorp.com
IDT Corporation	IDTC	www.idt.net
Interliant, Inc.	INIT	www.interliant.com
Internet Gold—Golden Lines Ltd.	IGLD	www.zahav.net.il
Internet Initiative Japan Inc.	IIJI	www.iij.ad.ip
ITXC Corp.	ITXC	www.itxc.com
Juno Online Services, Inc.	JWEB	www.juno.com
Log On America, Inc.	LOAX	www.loa.com
Mail.com, Inc.	MAIL	www.mail.com
MindSpring Enterprises, Inc.	MSPG	www.mindspring.net
Net2Phone, Inc.	NTOP	www.net2phone.com

(continued on next page)

Company Name	Ticker Symbol	Web Site
NetZero, Inc.	NZRO	www.netzero.com
NorthPoint Communications Holdings, Inc.	NPNT	www.northpointcom.com
OneMain.com, Inc.	ONEM	www.onemain.com
Pacific Internet Pte Ltd	PCNTF	www.pacific.net.sg
Prodigy Communications Corporation	PRGY	www.prodigy.com
ProtoSource Corporation	PSCO	www.protosource.com
PSINet Inc.	PSIX	www.psi.net
Rhythms NetConnections Inc.	RTHM	www.rhythms.net
RMI.NET, Inc.	RMII	www.rmi.net
Satyam Infoway Limited	SIFY	www.satyam.net.in
SPEEDUS.COM, INC.	SPDE	www.speedus.com
Splitrock Services, Inc.	SPLT	www.splitrock.com
Verio Inc.	VRIO	www.verio.com
Voyager.net, Inc.	VOYN	www.voyager.net
WorldGate Communications, Inc.	WGAT	www.wgatecom
ZapMe! Corporation	IZAP	www.zapme.com

Internet and online content providers (Courtesy of Hoover's Online, www.hoover.com)

Company Name	Ticker Symbol	Web Site
About.com, Inc.	BOUT	www.about.com
Actfit.com	ACTFF	www.actfit.com
Alloy Online, Inc.	ALOY	www.alloyonline.com
America Online, Inc.	AOL	www.aol.com
Ask Jeeves, Inc.	ASKJ	www.ask.com
Audible, Inc.	ADBL	www.audible.com
audiohighway.com	AHWY	www.audiohighway.com
BarPoint.com, Inc.	BPNT	www.barpoint.com
BoysToys.com	GRLZ	www.boystoys.com
China.com Corporation	CHINA	www.china.com
The Cobalt Group, Inc.	CBLT	www.cobaltgroup.com

(continued on next page)

Company Name	Ticker Symbol	Web Site
Crosswalk.com Inc.	AMEN	www.crosswalk.com
Cybear, Inc.	CYBA	www.cybear.com
Digital Courier Technology	DCTI	www.dcourier.com
DME Interactive Holding	DGMF	www.digitalmafia.com
drkoop.com, Inc.	KOOP	www.drkoop.com
EarthWeb Inc.	EWBX	www.earthweb.com
fashionmall.com, Inc.	FASH	www.fashionmall.com
FinancialWeb.com, Inc.	FWEBE	www.financialweb.com
foreignTV.com, Inc.	FNTV	www.foreigntv.com
GHS, Inc.	GHSI	www.anthonyrobbins.com
Global Business	GBDI	www.bizfiles.com
GoTo.com, Inc.	GOTO	www.goto.com
Go2Net, Inc.	GNET	www.go2net.com
HearMe.com	HEAR	www.hearme.com
Hitsgalore.com, Inc.	HITT	www.hitsgalore.com
Hoover's, Inc.	HOOV	www.hoovers.com
Infonautics, Inc.	INFO	www.infonautics.com
InfoSpace.com, Inc.	INSP	www.infospace.com
Intelligent Life Corporation	ILIF	www.bankrate.com
Internet.com Corporation	INTM	www.Internet.com
iTurf Inc.	TURF	www.iturf.com
Kanakaris Communication	KKRS	www.kanakaris.com
Launch Media, Inc.	LAUN	www.launch.com
Loislaw.com, Inc.	LOIS	www.loislaw.com
LookSmart, Ltd.	LOOK	www.looksmart.com
Lycos, Inc.	LCOS	www.lycos.com
Medscape, Inc.	MSCP	www.medscape.com
National Information Company	EGOV	www.nicusa.com
Netivation.com, Inc.	NTVN	www.netivation.com
NetRadio Corporation	NETR	www.netradio.com
NewsEdge Corporation	NEWZ	www.newsedge.com
OnHealth Network Company	ONHN	www.onhealth.com
On2.com Inc.	ONT	www.on2.com
Preview Travel, Inc.	PTVL	www.previewtravel.com
Priceline.com Corporation	PCLN	www.priceline.com
PTN Media, Inc.	PTNM	www.ptnmediainc.om

(continued on next page)

Company Name	Ticker Symbol	Web Site
PurchasePro.com, Inc.	PPRO	www.purchasepro.com
quepasa.com, inc.	PASA	www.quepasa.com
Quokka Sports, Inc.	QKKA	www.quokka.com
Salon.com	SALN	www.salon.com
Scoot.com plc	SCOP	www.scoot.com
Source Media, Inc.	SRCM	www.sourcemedia.com
Stan Lee Media, Inc.	SLEE	www.stanleemedia.com
StarMedia Network, Inc.	STRM	www.starmedia.com
Starnet Communication	SNMM	www.snmm.com
Stockscape.com Technology	STKSF	www.stockscape.com
Talk City, Inc.	TCTY	www.talkcity.com
Telescan, Inc.	TSCN	www.telescan.com
theglobe.com, inc.	TGLO	www.theglobe.com
TheStreet.com, Inc.	TSCM	www.thestreet.com
Ticketmaster Online—Citysearch Online	TMCS	www.ticketmaster.com
Town Pages Net.com plc	TPN	www.townpages.co.uk
VerticalNet, Inc.	VERT	www.verticalnet.com
Women.com Networks, Inc.	WOMN	www.women.com
WordCruncher Internet	WCTI	www.wordcruncher.com
World InterNetWorks, Inc.	WINW	www.wiworks.com
Xoom.com, Inc.	XMCM	www.xoom.com
Yahoo! Inc.	YHOO	www.yahoo.com
ZDNet Group	ZDZ	www.zdnet.com

Internet and Intranet software and services (Courtesy of Hoover's Online, www.hoovers.com)

Company Name	Ticker Symbol	Web Site
Accrue Software, Inc.	ACRU	www.accrue.com
Akami Technologies, Inc.	AKAM	www.akami.com
Allaire Corporation	ALLR	www.allaire.com
Alpha Microsystems	ALMI	www.alphamicro.com
Artifical Life, Inc.	ALIF	www.artificial-life.com

(continued on next page)

Company Name	Ticker Symbol	Web Site
The Ashton Technology Group, Inc.	ASTN	www.ashtontechgroup.com
BackWeb Technologies Ltd.	BWEB	www.backweb.com
Bluestone Software, Inc.	BLSW	www.bluestone.com
BroadVision, Inc.	BVSN	www.broadvision.com
Calico Commerce, Inc.	CLIC	www.calicocommerce.com
Cyber Merchants Exchange, Inc.	CMEE	www.c-me.com
CyberCash, Inc.	CYCH	www.cybercash.com
CyberSource Corporation	CYBS	www.cybersource.com
Cysive, Inc.	CYSV	www.cysive.com
Data Return Corporation	DRTN	www.datareturn.com
Digital Insight Corporation	DGIN	www.digitalinsight.com
Elcom International, Inc.	ELCO	www.elcominternational.com
Exodus Communications, Inc.	EXDS	www.exodus.net
ExperTelligence, Inc.	EXGP	www.webbase.com
F5 Networks, Inc.	FFIV	www.f5.com
Harbinger Corporation	HRBC	www.harbinger.com
Healtheon Corporation	HLTH	www.healtheon.com
HealthWatch, Inc.	HEAL	no www address
HomeCom Communications, Inc.	HCOM	www.homecom.com
I/NET, Inc.	INNI	www.inetmi.com
Inktomi Corporation	INKT	www.inktomi.com
Internet Commerce Corporation	ICCSA	www.icc.net
InterTrust Technologies Corporation	ITRU	www.intertrust.com
InterVU Inc.	ITVU	www.intervu.com
InterWorld Corporation	INTW	www.interworld.com
Intraware, Inc.	ITRA	www.intraware.com
Liberate Technologies	LBRT	www.liberate.com
Liquid Audio, Inc.	LQID	www.liquidaudio.com
MessageMedia, Inc.	MESG	www.messagemedia.com
Micro-Integration Corporation	MINT	www.miworld.com
N2H2, Inc.	NTWO	www.n2h2
NAVIDEC, Inc.	NVDC	www.navidec.com
NetObjects, Inc.	NETO	www.netobjects.com
NetUSA, Inc.	NTSA	www.netusa.com
Network Solutions, Inc.	NSOL	www.netsol.com
nFront, Inc.	NFNT	www.nfront.com

(continued on next page)

Company Name	Ticker Symbol	Web Site
Object Design, Inc.	ODIS	www.odi.com
Online Resources & Communications Corporation	ORCC	www.orcc.com
Open Market, Inc.	OMKT	www.openmarket.com
Open Text Corporation	OTEX	www.opentext.com
PC-Tel, Inc.	PCTI	www.pctel.com
Persistence Software, Inc.	PRSW	www.persistence.com
Primus Knowledge Solutions, Inc.	PKSI	www.primus.com
Proxicom, Inc.	PXCM	www.proxicom.com
RADWARE Ltd	RDWR	www.radware.com
RealNetworks, Inc.	RNWK	www.real.com
Security First Technologies Corporation	SONE	www.s1.com
Segue Software, Inc.	SEGU	www.segue.com
Silknet Software.com, Inc.	SILK	www.silknet.com
Software.com, Inc.	SWCM	www.software.com
Spyglass, Inc.	SPYG	www.spyglass.com
Telemate.Net Software, Inc.	TMNT	www.telemate.net
Unify Corporation	UNFY	www.unify.com
Viador Inc.	VIAD	www.viador.com
The viaLink Company	IQIQ	www.vialink.com
Vignette Corporation	VIGN	www.vignette.com
Webb Interactive Services, Inc.	WEBB	www.ossinc.net

MAIN POINTS TO REMEMBER

- The multitude of different stocks available allows you to diversify your holdings any way you desire.

- The key is to get in the habit of investing routinely—and starting *today!*

- Having a certain portion of your investments in stocks in the spotlight is a good way to maximize your investment capital.

6

ONLINE INVESTING STRATEGIES

SETTING INVESTMENT GOALS

Every online investor has different goals for his or her investments. With online investing, you can put your money in exactly the same investments you would with a traditional broker—right from the comfort of your computer. One of the best parts of online investing is that everything you could possibly invest in is right in front of you. It is just up to you to determine which investments are best for you. Regardless of whether you are saving to buy a house, pay for college, or plan for retirement, online investing presents a plethora of different options for every type of investor. The key is to determine your goals from the onset and invest in the right choices that will help you achieve those goals. Online investment firms are very user-friendly when it comes to walking you through the different investment options, and most even have a technical support line where you can call and talk to someone.

Many individuals jump into investing without any clear-cut plan. Although investing at any level is worthwhile, having a strategy greatly increases your ability to grow your capital. Even if you have already been investing for 20 years, it is always a good idea to revisit your goals on an annual basis (at the minimum). Especially with the incredible number of new stocks available to invest in, the opportunities now are greater than they have ever been. No matter what stage of investing you are currently at, it is always wise to outline exactly what it is you are saving for—whether for one particular thing or ten different things. Outlining your investment goals will help you understand how much you should be saving and how passively or aggressively you should be investing.

DOING YOUR HOMEWORK

Every investor is looking to make money, and each stock has a different level of risk associated with it. Those investors who do their homework on particular stocks instead of just buying a stock on a "hot tip" tend to do much better. Online investing presents unprecedented ways for any investor to research a stock. The Internet contains a wealth of information on almost every investment choice, and it is up to you to find the information that is important to you. Later, in Chapter 8, we point you to some of the best web sites to find this information so you can spend less time searching and more time studying. This is one of the major reasons online investors have an advantage over someone using a broker. Brokers get their information from the same sources as what's available on the Internet. In addition, brokers normally have many clients, so it is impossible for them to follow every one of your stocks and compare them to your personal goals. It is easier for you to spend a set amount of time each week looking at your stocks—and you'll pay significantly lower commissions. Why should you pay five to ten times as much to place a trade with a traditional broker when the information for you to invest successfully is available at any time, from any computer, and at a lower cost? The decision is very simple once you know where to look for this information and get comfortable spending some time researching your investments.

No matter what type of investor you are, it is important that you buy stocks that you are comfortable with. It is extremely important to understand about the company: how it is positioned for the future, and how its stock price has performed over the last number of years. A company's web site is one of the best places to go to find this information. Almost every business now has a web site, and it often contains a wealth of information that gives prospective investors, customers, and competitors a general overview of the company. Although you expect most of the information on the site to be very flattering, you can learn about upcoming plans by reading a company's press releases, and you can understand what type of experience the management team has by reading the biographies of the people on it.

After looking at a company's web site, it is a good idea to go to a more objective source to research the stock. Research reports are always an excellent source for unbiased views of how a company is performing. It is also a good idea to look at a company's competitors to understand what the company is doing differently and if it is well positioned for the future. Every individual has a different view on if and why a stock will do well; however, it is up to you to come up with your own reasons. There is so much to consider that it is often very difficult to accurately predict a stock's course every time. However, once you have a strategy you are comfortable with, investing becomes that much easier.

RESEARCH

There are many different ways to decide which stocks to invest in. Some of the most successful investors, such as Peter Lynch, have always said to invest in what you know. A lot of people are more comfortable investing in companies that are familiar to them. Other individuals are looking for the next hot technology stock that will make them a lot of money in a hurry. There are many different ways to decide which stock to invest in. The key is being comfortable with your investments. There are certain rules of thumb to stocks within a specific industry. Technology stocks tend to be much riskier investments than blue-chip stocks that have been around longer, such as Coca-Cola, Ford, and GE, and which tend to be a lot more stable. Every stock is prone to general market sentiment, but certain ones are much more prone to fluctuation. Fortunately, the Internet allows you to access a wealth of information on every stock and the ability to invest your money online as actively or passively as you desire.

There are two basic ways to research a stock: using technical analysis and using fundamental analysis. Technical analysis is when you study the way a stock has moved over time, using tools such as charts. It is very easy to determine which stocks have been more volatile by simply looking at a chart of their stock price. You can do this at financial web sites such as Hoover's (www.hoovers.com) and Big Charts (www.bigcharts.com) by just pulling up the chart of a particular stock. The chart will show you the price of the stock over any given time period. Fundamental analysis is determining how general market news will affect a stock's price. Fundamental analysis is based primarily on market news and the quality of the product or service the company is offering, whereas technical analysis examines how high or low the stock price is and whether it is poised to make a move. There are investors who only use fundamental or technical analysis; however, most investors use some combination of the two. Online investing allows you to virtually accumulate all the information you could possibly ever want on any stock to be able to analyze the stock any way you choose.

There has never been an easier and quicker way to research a stock. The Internet allows you to find almost any piece of information about a stock in a matter of seconds. As we mentioned before, the key is knowing where to go so that you maximize your time spent researching your investments. It is very easy to get lost for hours in cyberspace. Knowing the right web sites to visit for information will greatly expedite your trip. All of the information brokers have been using for years is now available—for free—on the Internet.

RISK LEVELS

Every investor has a different comfort level with risk. Depending on your financial situation and stage of life, you are going to want to invest in a way that allows you to have a varying degree of financial risk. Fortunately, online investing presents you with more investing opportunities than you probably ever knew existed. Instead of your broker having to tell you what is available, you can go online and take a look for yourself. Whether you like to invest in big companies such as GE and IBM or you prefer to take part in the initial public offerings (IPOs) of stocks, there are investment opportunities for everyone.

It is important to keep in mind that the market as a whole is subject to a certain level of risk. Even in a bull market, stocks are prone to go down at times, and there is no telling when a bull market will turn into a bear market. Fortunately, online investing presents you with the best tools possible to enter and exit trades at your will. There is no waiting to find out if your broker sold your stock for you and at what price. You simply turn on your computer, go to the web site of your online brokerage firm, place your order, and a couple of seconds later you have confirmation. If a stock is rapidly declining on a given day and you wish to exit your position, you will be in a much better position to take care of it yourself than to wait for someone else. Also, there are email alerts and extensive research available so that you can examine each individual stock and prevent delays from your broker when finding information for you. Although there is risk to buying any stock, having all of the information to research at your fingertips mitigates your risk. Online investing gives you the opportunity to do things your way instead of relying on the subjectivity of someone else who has more than just you as a client.

There is no denying that investing has a certain level of risk because you are giving other people control of your money hoping that they will use it to create even more money. Online investing is no more risky than investing with a traditional broker. As we discussed earlier, online safety precautions can easily be taken, and you can be assured of the safety of each of your trades. In addition, online investing gives you as much or as little control over your investments as you want. It is like having your own "robot broker" available to provide you with information 24 hours a day, 7 days a week. Online investing gives you the opportunity to mitigate some of the risks, but no matter how you invest, you need to be aware of certain market- and stock-specific risks.

DIVERSITY

One of the best ways to lower your overall risk is by investing in a variety of stocks. Each individual stock is subject to a certain amount of industry and general market risk; however, by owning a variety of stocks you can lower your overall risk. For example, one way to diversify your portfolio is to own some stocks in a more volatile industry such as technology as well as own more stable stocks in an industry such as the energy industry. Small-cap stocks, with a market capitalization of less than $500 million, will often fluctuate more than mid-cap stocks, having a market capitalization between $500 million and $5 billion, and large-cap stocks, defined as having a market capitalization greater than $5 billion. The market capitalization of a stock is determined by multiplying the number of shares outstanding by the current market price. The general rule of thumb is that the higher the price and the more shares outstanding, the less a stock will fluctuate. Stocks will always fluctuate up and down over the course of time; however, by having the right combination you put yourself in a more conservative position. Many people are certain that technology and other fast-growth stocks are the place to be, so they have all their money in that particular sector. Their reasoning is that even if a bunch of their other stocks go down, the one or two that really go up will more than make up for it. Although this is not always the case, many aggressive investors are placing bets such as these. Depending on your risk tolerance levels, it makes the most sense for people to diversify on some level.

MAKING MONEY WITH ONLINE INVESTING

Online investing gives you the chance to take advantage of an opportunity immediately. If you see that Dell is trading at 40 and that it has been as high as 43 earlier in the week and as high as 56 in the last four months, you may think this is an ideal opportunity to buy. However, for every second you spend on the phone with your broker explaining your order, your opportunity to buy at that price is changing. In addition, after you explain your order, your broker will have to fill out the paperwork and then call his or her representative to actually buy the stock. Filling your order can take minutes or even hours. With online investing, you can make it happen in a matter of minutes or even seconds. Online investing is an empowering tool for investors. For the first time it is possible for the individual investor to have access to the full spectrum of stock opportunities. Although these opportunities have been available in the past, there has been no way for individuals to get enough information on the stocks or be privy to the new "hot" stocks that brokers would save for their favorite (i.e., spend the most money with them) clients. Online investing levels the playing field and gives everyone the same opportunities to make money in the stock market.

The key to making money with online investing is identifying your investment goals, assessing the level of risk you are comfortable with, and determining how active you want to be with your account. Online investing suits the needs of everyone from a day trader to someone who may make only one investment in his or her lifetime. It does not matter how much money you have to invest or

the frequency at which you are going to make trades; online investing gives each investor the opportunity to take part in the stock market. Even if you make only one trade every five years, you will be
able to monitor it as frequently or infrequently as you desire, analyze
how the investment has made or lost money over time, and read
research by top Wall Street analysts. Everyone's investment goals
change over time, and online investing gives you the opportunity to
change them as often as you like. With so many investment opportunities available, you can change your portfolio whenever you desire.

There are many people who have made and lost a lot of money
from investing. Although some of these investors were wise and
bought IBM at $10 a share, many were the fortunate recipients of
insider advice from Wall Street professionals. Online investing has
unleashed the wave of information that used to be available only to
the big brokerage firms and Wall Street professionals. It used to be
extremely difficult to find out any information on a stock unless you
sorted through the wave of difficult-to-understand information in a
company's quarterly (10q) and annual (10k) reports. Now, any individual investor can go online and look up a particular stock and find
out just as much information about it as anyone else. There are
research reports, stock summaries, charts, and a plethora of other
information available on the Internet. There is so much information
available on the Internet that the brokers themselves now use it as
their most frequently used tool to research a stock. In addition, online
investors can find out about upcoming IPOs or whether a stock is
going to split—many times even before their broker knows. Online
investing puts the tools to make money in your hands. No longer do
you need to rely on someone else who may not always have your
best interests as a top priority.

TYPES OF INVESTING

Online investing allows you to be any type of investor on any given
day. Most people embody characteristics of a lot of different types of

investors over a given time period. At times they tend to be more long-term oriented; at other points they may be more aggressive. Defining your investment goals points you in the right direction for the types of stocks you should be investing in. Because online investing provides you with such a wide array of investment opportunities, it is possible to change your investment strategies at any point you choose. However, by defining your type of investing, you will be able to allocate which portions to devote to certain types of investing and maximize your capital while also avoiding any unnecessary risk.

Each investor has different investment goals and, therefore, should own a different mix of stocks. Being an online investor allows you to incorporate as many of these investing styles as you choose—and change them as often as you like. Everything is available to you online 24 hours a day, 7 days a week, 52 weeks a year. At the end of this chapter, we take a look at four different profiles of investors and examine the thoughts behind their investing strategies. Although no one profile may fit you exactly, you will be able to get an understanding of how to think through your current situation when identifying your investment strategy.

INVESTING STRATEGIES CONCLUSIONS

Every person is bound to have a different strategy for investing online. The key is to find a strategy that you are comfortable with and that works well for you. There are so many different investment options available that it is most important to invest in stocks that you are familiar with. With the wealth of information available online, it is possible to learn as much as you desire on any given company or industry. Take advantage of this information to broaden your knowledge base, and learn about other industries that interest you as well. Online investing allows you to be any type of investor you choose. There is no more choosing the best of three stocks your broker told you about, which you couldn't research even if you chose to. Online investing is an empowering tool for the individual investor. Use it to take full advantage of your investment dollars and capitalize on the amazing opportunities in the stock market.

SAMPLE INVESTOR PROFILES

RICHARD SAMS
(Novice Internet User, Beginner Investor, Age 40)

Richard has had very little experience using the Internet, let alone investing in general. He is extremely concerned about security issues and has used a computer only a number of times. He has had his money with his broker for the last 15 years. Although the market in general has experienced unrivaled growth over the last couple of years, Richard's investments have achieved only mediocre returns. He now feels it is time to take over his finances. Richard's broker has had him in a variety of mutual funds but has never really explained his reasoning for investing in these funds. Richard is committed to finally learning what it takes to invest and wants to use the Internet to do so. He is also very concerned about losing money and wants to find investment resources that will walk him through the basics of learning to invest.

CONCLUSION

The first thing Richard needs to do is to get himself a computer if he does not already have one. Although Richard could invest online by having access to a computer to make his trades, it is much better to have his own so that he can get more comfortable using the computer in general. Richard can go to PC Mall (www.pcmall.com), CDW (www.cdw.com), or

Value America (www.va.com) to purchase a computer for under $1,200 that will have enough memory and speed. After getting his computer, Richard will need to get Internet access. He can sign up for America Online (www.aol.com), Mindspring (www.mindspring.com), or even a new free Internet service provider such as Net Zero (www.netzero.com). All three will also provide him with an email address. Both AOL and Mindspring cost anywhere from $15 to $20 a month, whereas Net Zero is free (although he will have to put up with the ads at the bottom of his screen). Because Richard has been on the computer and the Internet only a couple of times, it is important for him to focus on a couple of web sites that are easy to use and will not overwhelm him with information. A great place for Richard to start is The Motley Fool (www.fool.com) for basic investment advice and content. That site will explain all aspects of investing to Richard and walk him through everything he needs to know to begin managing his investments. For an online broker, Richard should look at Ameritrade (www.ameritrade.com), TD Waterhouse (www.tdwaterhouse.com), or Firstrade (www.firstrade .com). All three of these online brokers have very easy-to-use graphical interfaces and excellent customer service. Richard will be able to ask questions via email or phone and have someone walk him through getting started and placing trades. In addition, all three place a heavy emphasis on security issues and will be able to reassure Richard as to the safety of his investments. By getting in a constant routine of surfing the Internet and managing his investments, Richard should be well on his way after a couple of sessions online.

WALT ABRAHMS
(Novice Internet User, Experienced Investor, Age 56)

Walt has limited experience using the Internet but has been investing for the last 30 years. He has been using a broker out of convenience and for the occasional "hot tip" he gets on a new stock offering, but he is very knowledgeable about what he wants to invest in. Walt has been unsure about the convenience and safety of using an online broker but is ready to start managing some of his investments online. He is seeking access to leading research and the ability to get in on some IPOs. If he enjoys the experience and gets more comfortable with online investing, he will think about transferring over more of his assets.

CONCLUSION

The first thing for Walt to do is to find a couple of web sites he is comfortable with. Because he is a more experienced investor, he will want to find sources of information that are easy to navigate yet have more advanced content-rich information. A great place for Walt to start is TheStreet.com (www.thestreet.com) and Hoover's (www.hoovers.com). TheStreet.com is a fantastic web site for more advanced investor information and breaking market news. TheStreet.com also has daily email alerts of breaking news that will keep Walt abreast of market activities throughout the course of the day. Hoover's is a great web site for Walt to do his own research on possible companies he may want to invest in. Hoover's presents summary information about a company (including financial statements) and also has an excellent IPO Corner for news about upcoming IPOs. Hoover's also has a weekly email that will keep Walt abreast

of all the top market happenings over the course of the
week. For an online broker, Walt should look at DLJdirect
(www.dljdirect.com), Wit Capital (www.witcapital.com),
and Morgan Stanley Dean Witter Online (www.online
.msdw.com). DLJdirect and Morgan Stanley Dean Witter
Online will both provide Walt with some of the best research
available anywhere, access to IPOs, and broker support if
needed. Wit Capital will provide Walt with access to IPOs,
private equity deals, and normal brokerage services. Walt
should spend some time on each site to see which one he
finds to be the easiest to use and provides him with the best
information to meet his needs. Because Walt has so much
experience with investing, once he takes the time to get
more comfortable on the Internet, he should be well on his
way to start managing all of his investments online.

JENNY GALSTON
(Intermediate Internet User, Intermediate Investor, Age 24)

Jenny, having recently been graduated from college and now
moving into the workforce, is looking to start "seriously"
investing. While in college she was able to invest $25 a
month into her Janus mutual fund, so she now has almost
$2,000 in investments. Because Jenny is fairly comfortable
on the Internet and has some limited experience with investing, it is important for her to find an online broker that will
be easy to use but that will also give her room to grow as she
explores other investment opportunities. Jenny wants to continue putting away a certain amount every month; however,
she wants to start investing in specific stocks. Because of her
busy schedule, she also wants to find an online broker that

can provide her with breaking news on the stocks that she invests in. Jenny is not looking for the high-flyer Internet stocks, but wants to start diversifying her stock mix with shares of blue-chip companies as well as more established technology companies.

CONCLUSION

There are a number of good online broker options for Jenny. She has some experience on the Internet and with investing, so it is a good idea for her to look at some of the online brokers that appeal to a wide range of investor types so that she has room to grow. Some good options for Jenny are E*TRADE (www.etrade.com), National Discount Brokers (www.ndb.com), and Siebert (www.msiebert.com). All three online brokers provide tools for all levels of the individual investor. E*TRADE especially will offer her the opportunity to receive email alerts regarding news on her specific stocks of interest and let her gain some experience with online investing with a mock investment game. Jenny would also be wise to begin using a site such as CBS MarketWatch for her research. CBS MarketWatch provides excellent unbiased content that will help her make her own investment decisions while providing her with enough guidance along the way. Because Jenny is just starting out in her investing, it is important to begin diversifying her investments. A web site such as CBS MarketWatch (www.marketwatch.com) will allow Jenny to learn about stocks that she currently owns in addition to new industries or specific stocks that may be of interest to her. As Jenny begins to get more comfortable with online investing, Siebert and E*TRADE will also allow her the opportunity to get in on IPOs, and NDB has some great educational content to improve her skills.

JAKE BURSTEIN
(Advanced Internet User, Advanced Investor, Age 32)

Jake has been investing for seven years now and is very aggressive in his investments. An avid IPO fan, he is looking for an online broker that will allow him to get in on some of the hot Internet offerings. The broker should also be geared toward active traders and provide special tools to actively monitor his account. Jake is also interested in all the hype surrounding day trading and may want to try it out. Even though Jake does not have a financial background, he has spent time analyzing the technology industry and is now ready to go online and start taking advantage of his knowledge. His broker returns his calls in two to three days and seems to never get him in on the IPOs he wants. Jake has been using the Internet for almost three years now but has been slow to make the jump to online investing because of the "personal attention" he thought he was getting from his broker. Jake has finally realized that the extra thousands of dollars he is spending every year on commissions can finally be put to a much better use—buying more shares of stock.

CONCLUSION

There are a number of goods ways for Jake to get started with online investing. Because he is an extremely active investor and has experience on the Internet, he would be happiest at a firm that provides all the tools for him to take control and which offered IPOs. Some potential online brokerage firms for Jake would be Wit Capital (www .witcapital.com), DLJdirect (www.dljdirect.com), and Tradescape.com (www.tradescape.com). Wit Capital, one of the pioneers in offering IPOs to the individual investor, currently has the largest number of IPOs but lacks some of the advanced monitoring tools for active traders. This could make an excellent second account for Jake to use solely for trying and getting in on IPOs. DLJdirect is another excellent potential online broker for Jake, provided that he has $100,000 in assets (required amount to get in on IPOs and equity research). DLJdirect combines the power of the investment banking firm Donaldson, Lufkin & Jenrette with online investing and provides some of the best tools for the experienced investors. Tradescape.com would allow Jake to get into day trading when he is ready to take that jump. Tradescape.com offers Nadsaq Level II quotes and their proprietary software Tradescape 1.0 to access the markets directly and eliminate any brokers or middlemen altogether. Most people do not realize that active online investors often have numerous accounts to take advantage of certain features (such as IPOs) offered by specific online brokers. Jake should also make sure to check out TheStreet (www.thestreet.com), which has excellent information for the more active and advanced investor.

MAIN POINTS TO REMEMBER

- Setting your investment goal on an annual or semi-annual basis is an important step in deciding which stocks to invest in.

- There will always be a certain level of risk to any type of investing, but by doing your homework and managing your account you will be able to greatly mitigate this risk.

- Anyone can make money with online investing—the tools are there. It is now up to you to take advantage of them.

CHAPTER 7

THE TRUTH ABOUT DAY TRADING

WHAT IS DAY TRADING?

Day trading is a way to take advantage of intra-day fluctuations within stocks. With the increased volatility in the markets, there is now the opportunity to make large amounts of money from entering and exiting positions within hours or even seconds. When you look at a newspaper, you will see where a stock closed for a particular day. However, what that quote does not tell you is that although the stock closed at 46, it was at one point up to 52 and as low as 43. Day traders look for highly volatile stocks and attempt to take advantage of their intra-day fluctuations. Over the last year, day trading has gained a lot of attention as a risky way to make a lot of money in the markets very quickly. However, day trading can provide lofty returns provided you have the right tools to succeed.

It is important to understand the difference between online investing and day trading. The confusion with day trading stems primarily from the fact that there are so many different types of day traders. There is no official license to become a day trader—anyone can do it. Although numerous online investors do day trade using their online broker, serious day traders use the technology that allows them to access the markets directly. Over the last couple of years, most day traders have been either joining an actual day trading firm where they have the proprietary direct access to the markets or trying to make the best of it using their online broker. Software has recently become available that allows anyone to day trade from any computer having an Internet connection and the software. By accessing the markets directly, you are essentially eliminating the middleman (your online broker) and trading directly with another party. Although the interface to do so is not nearly as friendly as for placing a trade with an online brokerage firm, it enables you to have immediate execution and capitalize on quick point moves. Day trading is not easy. It takes time to learn how to interpret the markets, and this time can often cost you a lot of money. Experienced day traders always recommend investing only the money that you can afford to lose—and giving yourself three to six months before you actually begin making any money. The technology behind day trading is already revolutionizing the world markets. It is only a matter of time before everyone will be using this technology on some level to trade directly with another party.

THE HISTORY OF DAY TRADING

Until recently it has been impossible for the normal investor to compete with the Wall Street professionals. This inner circle has been slow to relinquish its advantages to the general public, but with recent advances made in technology and deregulation by the SEC, individual investors can now compete with the big boys. It was previously impossible for an individual not associated with a big trading firm to gain access to the necessary tools to trade successfully. Only the large firms could afford the technology necessary to capitalize on time-sensitive information and access the markets directly. However, technology has bridged the gap between the large brokerage firms and individual investors and has created a more level playing field, much to the dismay of the Wall Street professionals.

The brokerage community has been slow to let go of its stranglehold on the markets. For a long time traditional brokers had been able to charge extremely high rates and keep their customers behind the curtain. The regulatory restrictions placed on brokerage firms in May 1975, infamously dubbed May Day, marked the end of fixed commissions. This set the stage for a new group of competitors, lower rates, and easier access to the markets for the individual investor. Then the SEC was able to finally make changes to level the playing field once and for all for individual investors. The biggest decision was the mandatory participation in the Small Order Execution System (SOES), which allowed customers to send their orders directly to the floor without the need for a middleman. With the progress made in technology and the ability to access the trading floor directly, individuals were able to trade with the same information as the professionals. The stage was now set for day traders to enter the scene.

There have been a number of circumstances leading to the rise of day trading. Over the last couple of years, general interest in the stock market has increased dramatically with the rise of the Internet industry. This interest has made many more individuals actively trade their account rather than sit back and hope to beat the Standard & Poor's average. The billions of dollars made from the creation of Internet companies have created a much more active and volatile market. Where it used to take stocks months if not years to move a fraction of their share price, Internet stocks have been known to double or triple in value on their first day of trading. It is now possible to be in a stock for just a matter of minutes and come away with a multi-point gain. These factors have drastically increased the activity in the markets and created a more volatile environment—the ideal environment for day traders.

For the first time, individual investors can now access the markets from their home or office using an online brokerage firm. Lower commissions, easier access to research, and the ability to take advantage of the amazing wealth being created by Internet stocks have caused an overall increase in the number of people actively managing their accounts. This increased interest in the stock market has led to more individuals seeking the same opportunities as Wall Street professionals. The number of individuals investing online has skyrocketed. For the online investors who want to take their skills to the next level, day trading has become the answer.

Although SOES was the original order execution system for day traders, ECNs have become the predominant way for day traders to execute trades. The best known ECNs are Instinet and Island. ECNs work like an order book where they match the buyers and sellers for particular stocks. As the markets have changed dramatically over the last couple of years, so has the technology traders and investors use to access the markets. As the stock market moves toward more of a direct model, ECNs will play a large part in shaping the future of the electronic markets.

OPPORTUNITIES

There are incredible opportunities to make substantial money day trading. Many people are unaware of how active stocks actually are during the course of a day, even if they did only close up ⅛ or down ¼. The increased volume of shares being traded has created a much more liquid and volatile market: therefore, it is easier for individuals to get into and out of a stock at a desired price. Day traders typically trade in 100-share increments and look for opportunities where they can make a quick gain in the market. Although every day trader's strategy is different, most look to exit losing positions as quickly as possible and let their winners ride.

The opportunity to make a lot of money day trading is directly proportional to the amount of risk an individual day trader is willing to take. Trading large amounts of stock greatly increases your ability to make more money; however, it also increases your risk. Most successful day traders look to make a couple of thousand dollars a day, with the occasional big day where they could make $50,000 to $100,000. Consistently making money day in and day out adds up in the long run. Those day traders who continuously go for home runs usually wind up in trouble very quickly. Even if you make a lot of money in the beginning, a couple of big risky trades can wipe it out in a hurry. Consistently placing conservative trades and sticking to a regimented strategy is the best way to remain a winner. The key is being patient.

The day trading craze has taken hold of Wall Street, and thousands of individuals are taking a shot. The day trading opportunity appeals to everyone from Wall Street professionals to college graduates with an English major. Some of the most successful day traders have never even taken a finance course. Day trading provides individuals with the opportunity to make a lot of money on their own terms. Especially on Wall Street, where most employees have to wait almost 20 years to make the big money and be in control, the opportunity is simply too tempting for many. The universal appeal of day trading is that anyone can do it, and if successful, you can become incredibly wealthy.

HOW TO DAY TRADE

There are many different ways to day trade, and there are many different types of day traders. Some individuals trade using their online broker, whereas others go into work every day at a day trading firm. Although the differences are substantial, you can day trade both ways. No matter which way you trade, you definitely need the capital to trade with. Some day trading firms will match the amount of capital you trade with, but then take a certain percentage of your profits. Each day trading method is suited for a certain type of trader. Determining whether to day trade using conventional online brokers or more sophisticated technology such as ECNs is the real question.

When investors place a trade with an online broker such as E*TRADE or Ameritrade, they are essentially using that firm as a broker. The firm taking the trade places the order with someone else who is willing to pay that price for the stock. There is also usually a couple of seconds or even minutes before the order is confirmed. This is essentially when the broker is looking for the person who will buy the stock at the given price. There is definitely a disadvantage to day trading using an online brokerage firm (although many people do this). Online brokers may be easier for day traders to use, but they do not provide direct access to the markets or the real-time information that is so crucial to succeed.

Professional day traders predominantly use ECNs to place their trades, thereby eliminating the middleman. Until recently, the technology available to access ECNs was available only at day trading firms. These firms are now starting to offer the software so that you can place trades from the comfort of your own home. Day traders pay a commission on every share traded, usually amounting to less than commissions charged by online brokerage firms.

Speed is critical to day trading. An opportunity may be there for only two or three seconds, and you must be able to react instantaneously. Therefore, in order to take advantage of these opportunities, it is extremely helpful to have a fast Internet connection such as a T1, T3, or DSL line. You also must learn to be quick on the keyboard. If you are placing trades over an ECN or SOES, the systems are not as user-friendly as an online brokerage firm (although your advantage is exponentially greater). There are also numerous ECNs, so you must be able to quickly determine which one to use. Island and Instinet are the biggest; others, however, are gaining in popularity. The key is to make your trades on the ECNs that have the most volume so that you will be able to find a buyer or seller instantaneously.

Getting comfortable with the methods of execution is the hardest part for most individuals who have been using an online brokerage firm to day trade. There are many more ways to place a trade than most people have ever realized. It takes very little training to get comfortable with the different ways to place a trade, and in the end the advantages far outweigh the new learning experience. Many day trading firms even offer training in the way of seminars or instruction manuals. The best teacher, however, is always a successful day trader. It cannot be put into words exactly what makes a successful day trader, but those who are successful have a distinct way of making money day in and day out. Listen and learn, but do not be afraid to put your own thoughts into the mix. It is critical for you to determine your own strategy instead of trying to mimic a successful day trader.

Start out practicing on a system with phantom positions. Almost all day trading and online brokerage firms offer simulation games where you can pretend you are trading without using real money. Practice like this for at least a couple weeks until you have a strategy you are comfortable with and you have made winning trades on a consistent basis. Day trading is very different than investing, and it will take time to become accustomed to the frenetic pace at which stocks move. With the hundreds of people buying and selling every second, every stock is in a continuous state of change. Stocks are usually their most active when the market opens at 9:30 and for the last half hour before it closes at 4:00. It is during these times that a stock can move more than at any other time of the day, thus providing the best opportunities for day traders.

When you do begin day trading, it is a good idea to start out in stocks that are not the most volatile. Look for stocks that may only have a two- to three-point spread (the range with which they trade) over the course of the day. This will minimize your risk and give you the feel for actually making real trades. Stocks such as Yahoo!, Amazon, and AOL are flooded with day traders trying to make money. Once you have improved your skills, you can start working with these stocks. Each day trader has a different strategy for the stocks he or she trades. Some trade only a handful of Internet stocks; others trade only stocks that are significantly less active. The key is to find the stocks you are comfortable working with.

No matter what level of day trading you undertake, it is always critical to do your homework. Showing up five minutes before the market opens and expecting to be ready to trade is very unrealistic. It is always a good idea to look at the stocks you are interested in trading and see if they have any news being released. Study your trades from the day before to see where you made good and bad trades. Which ones should you have held onto longer or sold sooner? Becoming a successful day trader is a continual learning process. Day traders who believe they have entirely uncovered the secrets of day trading are doomed to failure. Day trading is very much like a sport where you must continuously practice (study the markets and the particular stocks you trade) to stay on top of your game.

DAY TRADING STRATEGIES

Day trading can be done on many levels. There are "professional" day traders who go to work every day at a day trading firm, share ideas with other day traders, and make trades from 9:30 to 4:00 every day. There are other individuals who use the software necessary to access the markets directly from the comfort of their home. Some day traders never leave their seats while the markets are open; others trade only for the hour the market opens and the hour before it closes. Every day trader has a different strategy. The key is finding one that you are comfortable with and that works.

Technology has enabled the individual investor to access the markets directly instead of having to place an order through a middleman. The advent of SOES, and more recently ECNs, allows individuals to access the markets in the same fashion as the Wall Street professionals. Only a couple of years ago, day traders were happy to make a ⅛ point or ¼ point on an individual trade and quickly move on to the next opportunity. They would often only be in a trade for a matter of seconds and scalp a quick profit off the top. Nowadays, with the increased volatility in the markets, it is possible for a stock to fluctuate a couple of points in a matter of seconds. Internet stocks have even moved up to triple their current value all in the course of one day. These types of opportunities have made many day traders multimillionaires, while making others lose their shirts. Beginners who come in expecting to make a killing immediately are prone to trouble. Nevertheless, day trading does require an extreme amount of confidence and self-belief. Even the best day traders are right only about 50 percent of the time, yet this is enough to make millions over the course of the year as long as winning stocks outperform losers. The most successful day traders are the ones who have discipline, can admit when they are wrong, and get out of a losing position early.

The markets are in a continuous state of change, and one of the greatest benefits of day trading is the ability to capitalize on opportunities while the market is going up or down. Many people incorrectly assume that if the market were to crash, it would be the end of day traders. In actuality, day traders would be in one of the best positions to make money as the market goes down. Armed with the ability to directly access the markets, they would be able to short stocks as they went down and then also buy them back at a much cheaper price. While someone is placing a trade with the traditional or online broker and waiting for confirmation, day traders are able to immediately execute their trades. In fact, day traders will attempt to short stocks as they go down and make money off of the panicked investors who will get out at any price. Day trading puts you in control and not dependent on someone else finding a buyer or seller for your security. Although a long-term bear market would not be good for anyone, day traders would be in one of the best positions to continue making money.

Many day traders actually know very little about a stock they are trading. Instead, they look more at volume and historical trading levels to determine where a stock is heading. Because stocks are only in a position for a very short period of time, this sort of analysis is much more accurate than basic fundamental analysis such as whether earnings will be up when they are released next week. Day traders also look to actively short stocks when they feel they are headed down. The only thing day traders need to make money is volatility. As long as a stock is moving up and down, day traders can judge market sentiment and make money just as easily as it goes up or as it goes down.

The most important difference between day trading and online investing is what individuals seek in the stock. Online investors are usually more interested in the company, earnings, and other fundamental news. Day traders look more closely at volume, historical levels, and market-maker activity. Many people find it difficult to train their mind to look for this new criterion when evaluating stocks. However, all of these factors play into what makes a stock move. Day traders try to understand the personality of a stock. What is it that makes it move? How has it reacted to a certain price level in the past? Why is it that Goldman Sachs keeps selling shares? These are just some of the questions that day traders must be able to answer in order to determine which way a stock is going to move. The markets are changing every day, which means that successful day traders adjust their strategies daily in order to keep up to date with market sentiment.

Every day trader has a different strategy. Some trade only IPOs, others trade only technology stocks, and some trade only less known (and less volatile) stocks. Some day traders watch hundreds of stocks, but others may watch only two or three. The strategies for each day trader are entirely dependent on the person's risk/reward profile. Discipline is the most important part of day trading, and those day traders who religiously follow their strategy over time have a much greater chance of succeeding. Strategies must be continuously updated, forcing a day trader to have discipline and requiring a lot of emotion in the process. The most successful day traders are those who methodically enter and exit trades based on predetermined criteria and continuously study their trades to learn from there mistakes.

The most important element is to keep your goals for day trading realistic. No matter how active a day trader you are going to be, you must clearly define your day trading strategy and your risk/reward profiles. If you are going to day trade only once in a while, you must be more realistic about the opportunities you are seeking. It is almost impossible to jump into a stock you have never watched before and make money on an intra-day basis.

RISKS

The amount of risk a particular day trader takes on is completely determined by his or her risk comfort level. Day traders are performing the exact same function as online investors. They are buying the stock at one price and then selling it back at another—although usually within a much shorter time period. For individuals who do not have the time to commit to day trading, the proposition is a lot riskier. So much of what successful day traders do is try to understand the personality of a stock and how it reacts to certain pieces of market news and at what levels it has traded in the past. Only by watching stocks day in and day out can one really start to get a feel for a stock. Some of the best day traders are able to trade for only an hour when the market opens and then an hour when the market closes because they understand the psychology of the masses so well. These tend to be the most active hours of the day, and day traders can do very well just by placing one or two winning trades in stocks they know extremely well.

The number one reason day traders fail is that they enter the field thinking it is going to be easy money. Day trading is hard work, just like any other profession. It takes time to experiment with different trading strategies and to get a good feeling for a couple of different stocks. Many day traders also come in trying to handle too much at once. So much of day trading is being able to interpret volatility, and attempting to monitor 300 stocks every day makes it impossible to get a good feeling for all of them. Also, many day traders start trading highly volatile stocks such as Yahoo and Amazon where the rewards and the risks are much higher. It is better to start off in stocks that will not move as much over the course of the day and get experience in executing trades. If you are using an ECN instead of an online broker, it is an entirely different experience. It takes time to learn the keyboard, understand the different methods of execution, and adjust your trading strategy. Day traders must be able to instinctively react to market opportunities and buy and sell on a second's notice.

There are inherently numerous risks associated with day trading; however, many of the risks are the same as if you were simply investing. The most important thing for any day trader or online investor is to determine a set strategy before beginning. For example, if you lose a certain amount of money on one particular position, you sell it and move on to another stock. Having a regimented strategy removes some of the emotion when a stock is going down and you hold onto it hoping it will go back up. If that stock hits a certain point, sell. The number one reason individuals lose so much money is that they wait for stocks to go back up. If you experiment with day trading, do not expect too much too quickly, be disciplined, and be realistic about your goals.

THE FUTURE OF DAY TRADING

Day trading has very quickly crept its way into the national spotlight. Unfortunately, for every story of someone becoming a millionaire, there is a story of someone losing his or her shirt. There is no question that people who go into day trading expecting to make millions immediately are doomed to failure. Becoming a successful day trader takes time and a willingness to lose some money in the beginning. There will always be day traders making money in the markets, and not just in stocks. The opportunities to day trade other securities will evolve in the near future. For those who have the ability to decipher market news, technical analyses, and consumer sentiment all in a matter of seconds, the challenge of day trading coupled with the opportunity to make a lot of money is an excellent opportunity.

Even though day trading may not be for everyone, the technology that day traders use will eventually be incorporated into every online investor's trading arsenal. The ability to access the markets directly and eliminate the middleman will become universal over time. The markets are moving toward much more of a direct model, and it is a matter of time before more and more individuals begin investing directly. Direct access to the markets means that in the near future individuals are going to be able to trade securities other than stocks directly with another party. The role of the broker or middleman is quickly disappearing, although they will wisely offer the services to help you trade directly as well. In addition, increased hours for trading will continue to generate additional interest in the markets. The interface for trading directly is still very confusing to most; however, over time it will become much easier to use, very similar to the way online investing was only a couple of years ago. The U.S. public has been kept in the dark for a long time with respect to how our financial markets actually work. With more and more people gaining direct access to the markets, the opportunities will continue to grow for those early adapters who understand what direct access can do. Although day trading may not be for everyone, the technology used to access the markets directly will eventually be used by all.

MAIN POINTS TO REMEMBER

- Day trading presents the opportunity to make money on intraday swings within a stock.
- Discipline is the most important aspect of day trading.
- Be realistic about your goals as a day trader.
- Determine a very clear-cut risk/reward strategy.
- The technology behind day trading will eventually be used by all.

8

AFTER-HOURS TRADING

WHAT IS IT?

After-hours trading is the ability to place orders both before the market opens and after it closes. When trading after hours, you bypass placing an order through a broker and make it directly with another individual who takes on the other side of your trade. After-hours trading is considered riskier than normal trading because of the possibilities for large price swings in an "inefficient market" that does not have enough buyers and sellers. After-hours trading is done through electronic communication networks (ECNs), which act like an order book, electronically matching buyers and sellers. Each ECN is its own distinct entity; a trade placed on one

ECN will not be seen on another. The general public is still very much in the dark regarding after-hours trading. Nevertheless, after-hours trading is just another step for online investors to be able to access the same tools at the Wall Street professionals.

After-hours trading has received a lot of attention recently because of the significant price swings of Internet and technology stocks due to news released after hours. Companies such as Dell and Microsoft have seen their stock prices rise and fall multiple points in after-hours trading. Wall Street professionals have had access to sell stocks after hours for a long time, but only recently has this power been bestowed on the individual investor. Advances made in investing technology such as ECNs make it possible for online investors to trade this way. Almost all of the top online brokerage firms are scrambling to form relationships with ECNs in order to offer some level of after-hours trading to their customers. As of July 1999, online brokerages have even started offering limited after-hours trading both before the market opens and after it closes. Although under intense scrutiny from the SEC, after-hours trading is spreading rapidly as individual investors continue to break down the walls between Wall Street professionals and themselves.

Most people take for granted that the markets open every day at 9:30 A.M. and close at 4:00 P.M. What they do not realize is that there is extensive trading done outside of these hours, especially on the Nasdaq, which is an electronically linked network, but also for stocks on the NYSE. Especially active are institutional traders and Wall Street professionals who often hold large blocks of stock and have the technology to be able to access the markets directly. They are able to respond when a company releases earnings, announces a stock split, or reports on any other information after hours. This can be very important especially in today's volatile markets. In the past, online investors had to wait until the market opened in order to enter or exit a position. Now, because of the Internet's ability to allow investors to communicate with an ECN via their online broker, online investors are beginning to place trades themselves after hours.

Advantages. After-hours trading provides online investors with their first taste of being able to eliminate the middleman and trade directly with another party. When trading after hours, you actually have the ability to see a lot more information regarding what is driving a particular stock price up or down. You will be able to see the different market makers trading the stock and at what price they are bidding to buy the stock—all information that you would not normally be able to see when placing a trade with your online broker.

So why don't online brokers usually show you this detailed information? Well, the answer is that the technology behind after-hours trading actually eliminates the need for brokers in general. Online brokers provide you with a snapshot of information, such as a quote and volume of shares being traded, so that you can make an informed trade. They are the ones who actively go into the marketplace and make the trade with a third party. Therefore, because the technology has now advanced so that you can trade directly with the other party, the online brokers are trying to create an interface that makes the technology easier to use. In its original state, it is very confusing and difficult to follow. What the online brokerages are doing is creating an easy-to-use interface so that online investors are comfortable with the new technology. The technology behind after-hours trading allows you to access even greater information when making an investment decision.

A perfect example of the advantage to after-hours trading is when a public company releases earnings or announces a stock split. Most companies wait until after the market is closed in order to prevent unnecessary volatility with their stock price. With after-hours trading, you have the ability to potentially get in at a much better price than the rest of the general public waiting for a stock to open the next morning. Technology stocks especially have been known to move a large number of points in after-hours trading when they announce important information. This can be a great way for you to take advantage of your newfound knowledge in placing the trade directly instead of waiting for the markets to open in the morning.

Risks. There are always going to be risks associated with investing, whether through a broker or on the Internet. The key is understanding those risks and taking active steps to mitigate them. In Chapter 2 we provided some very easy ways to make your online investing experience even safer than investing with a traditional broker. After-hours trading presents many of the same risks as online investing with some additional ones. The technology behind after-hours trading is new. It is just as safe as any other part of online investing; however, a lot of the terminology will be new to you and the graphical interface will not be as user-friendly as you are used to. As the technology advances, there will be more and more ways to learn about it, and it will also become easier to use.

After-hours trading is riskier in the sense that there are not as many buyers and sellers to take the opposite end of your trade. Because you are using ECNs, and each ECN is its own distinct entity, there will be a much lower level of volume. This will also mean that the spreads between what you buy the stock at and what you sell it at will generally be wider. Quotes obtained will only represent the current available prices on that particular ECN. ECNs are almost like their own mini-stock exchanges; therefore, it is entirely possible that is could be less or more expensive on another ECN. It is also important to keep in mind that currently many after-hours traders are institutions or professional traders.

WHOM IS IT FOR?

After-hours trading will eventually be used by everyone as we head toward a global financial marketplace that is open at all times to all investors. Right now, however, after-hours trading should be used predominantly by the advanced and/or active investor who is interested in taking advantage of new investing technology. More and more activity is occurring outside of market hours, and there are clearly profits to be made from after-hours trading. It is also interesting to note that many individuals on the West Coast particularly are getting into after-hours trading (their current market hours are from 6:30 A.M. to 1:00 P.M.). Although the market tends not to fluctuate as much after hours, there are certain cases where stocks can be very volatile. Also, in after-hours trading there are not as many buyers and sellers that make for a less efficient market. Therefore, it is extremely important to have realistic expectations about after-hours trading. After-hours trading is still in its infancy, and individual investors are getting their first glimpse at the future of investing technology.

The technology behind after-hours trading is currently used primarily by day traders. They use this technology to be able to make profits from trades that they enter and exit, often several times within minutes. Because they have access to this extra level of information, they can see the momentum driving the stock and make a fast $\frac{1}{16}$ or $\frac{1}{8}$ point very quickly. Although your investing goal may not be to make intra-day trades, there is no reason why you should not get the best price possible. This technology allows you to do that, once you understand the information being presented to you and how to use it. This takes some time to learn and get comfortable with, although the information is really no more complicated than what you use right now—just more in depth.

THINGS TO KEEP IN MIND

When trading after hours, there are a couple of key points to keep in mind that will make your trading experience better.

- *Liquidity.* Because there are fewer individuals trading after hours, the liquidity is going to be that much less. This lack of liquidity can mean there is a greater chance of your trade not being executed. Most online brokerages offering after-hours trading automatically cancel your order if it has not been fulfilled by the end of the after-hours trading session.

- *Price.* With the lower volume of shares being traded, there tends to be a wider price fluctuation and wider spreads between buyers and sellers. In addition, because you are trading on one ECN, it is possible that the stock is trading at a completely different price on another ECN.

- *Breaking news.* Because most companies release earnings and other news after market hours, there is a chance for an extreme fluctuation in price. It is a good idea to find out what companies may be releasing news before the after-hours trading session. Remember that most after-hours traders are part of institutions or Wall Street professionals; therefore, it is very important to do your homework and not just jump into the after-hours trading market.

- *Quotes.* After-hours quotes obtained through your online broker represent the price for the stock only through their specific ECN. It is entirely possible that you would be able to find a better or worse price on another ECN. It is also possible that the market may open the following morning at another price on the Nasdaq or NYSE.

- *Order types.* Online brokerages currently offering after-hours trading are placing much greater restrictions on orders than normal orders placed when the markets are open. For example, most online brokers only accept limit orders in round lots (multiples of 100) of shares during after-hours trading.

PLACING AN AFTER-HOURS TRADE

Placing an after-hours trade is very similar to placing a normal brokerage trade, with two major exceptions. First, there is no one officially "brokering" the trade; you are directly buying or selling a security to another individual. Second, you will be able to see a lot more information than you are probably used to. You will essentially be able to see the inside market of a particular stock and see the buyers and sellers pushing the stock up and down. Almost all of the big online brokers, such as E*TRADE, Datek, and Schwab, offer some level of after-hours trading. However, after-hours trading features are different on each online broker. In addition, new players such as Tradescape.com serve as an execution service only, not an online broker. The following descriptions highlight the different features of each service.

E*TRADE. On E*TRADE you can only trade after hours from 4:05 P.M. to 6:30 P.M. Eastern Time. The commissions are exactly the same as for trades executed during normal market hours. E*TRADE offers after-hours trading through the Instinet ECN, which is one of the largest ECNs representing more than 90 percent of the institutional equity funds and accounting for nearly 20 percent of the Nasdaq dialing trading volume. In order to qualify for after-hours trading on E*TRADE, you must agree to its Real-Time Exchange Agreement. You can only place limit orders in after-hours trading, and it has a special area for after-hours quotes from Instinet. Investors can only place limit orders for stocks traded on the NYSE or Nasdaq market, and those orders are only good until the end of the after-hours trading session (6:30 P.M.).

Datek. Datek was the first of the online brokers to offer after-hours trading. Datek offers after-hours trading both before the market opens in the morning from 8:00 A.M. until 9:30 A.M. Eastern Time and after the market closes from 4:00 P.M. until 8:00 P.M. Eastern Time. Datek offers after-hours trading through the Island ECN, in which it has a proprietary interest. Only Nasdaq stocks are available for trading during extended-hours trading, and investors must register for their account to have access. Investors can access the Island Book Viewer for a wealth of information on any stock traded there. The Island Book Viewer displays information such as whether an order is a buy or sell, the price, the quantity of shares being traded, and the activity within the specific stock. It is an incredibly powerful tool because it enables you to see what is going on "behind the scenes" within a particular stock. It allows you to see how the momentum from the various players is driving the stock in a particular direction. It is important to note, however, that you are seeing buy and sell orders for the Island ECN only. Therefore, as on any other ECN, you have a much smaller snapshot of what is happening in the market that can lead to bigger spreads and more exposure for you personally.

Schwab. Schwab, currently the largest online broker, recently unveiled its after-hours trading service to its online investors. The Schwab after-hours trading is done through the REDIBook ECN, and the fees are comparable to its standard commission schedule. Individuals can place an order from 4:05 P.M. to 7:00 P.M. Eastern Time, Monday through Friday, but the order will not be executed until the official opening of Schwab's after-hours trading session at 4:30 P.M. Orders can be placed online or by calling a toll-free number and speaking with an after-hours trading representative. Schwab only permits limit orders and short sell limit orders after hours, with all orders being in increments of 100 shares up to the maximum order size of 5,000 shares.

Tradescape.com. Tradescape.com is one of the newest players to begin offering direct access to the markets for online investors. It has developed an Internet-based software, Tradescape 1.0, which allows users to simultaneously view real-time Nasdaq information on their screen, including Level II quotes, a position manager, and an intraday chart. The key to Tradescape.com is that its software can be used during normal market hours as well as after hours. The technology behind Tradescape.com routes orders to the best price execution instantaneously and provides direct access to the Nasdaq, NYSE, and

ECNs. Because Tradescape.com is for the more advanced traders, it also offers a plethora of other features that cannot yet be accessed at an online brokerage. Currently, most users of Tradescape.com are day traders; however, many individuals are starting to use Tradescape .com simply for its advanced technology and ability to trade with this information at all times. Tradescape.com currently charges $79.99 a month and $1.50 per 100 shares traded.

Although online brokers do not offer any extensive education regarding after-hours trading, they do walk you through some of the basics you need to get started. As the SEC continues to investigate after-hours trading, watch for expanded educational material for the individual investor. Moreover, there will be execution services that provide the same tools of after-hours trading at all times during the day. As the world heads toward a truly global financial marketplace that is "open" at all hours, online brokers will be the ones many of us use to access this new world of information.

ECNS

An ECN is a computerized trading network used to match buy and sell orders. Wall Street professionals have been using ECNs for over 15 years to directly access the markets. In 1997, Nasdaq added ECNs to its automated quotations system, and quotes and sizes were finally posted on ECNs.

On an ECN, you can enter an order at any price, although for the transaction to be executed someone else has to take the other end of the trade. ECNs are growing in popularity, but because each one is different, they pose a little steeper learning curve for new users.

Archipelago. Archipelago, one of the four originally approved ECNs, allows participants to interact simultaneously with all Nasdaq ECNs and market makers. Archipelago employs a fairly user-friendly point-and-click order entry to ensure speed and accuracy for its customers (currently market-maker firms, professional traders, and institutional clients). Though not Internet based, Archipelago uses the Internet as a network and is Windows 95 and Windows NT compatible. Recent investors Goldman Sachs and E*TRADE are betting that Archipelago will be one of the leaders in the future of electronic trading.

The Island. The Island ECN, owned by Datek Online Holdings, has some of the best volume for after-hours traders. Island displays your order to its vast network of subscribers and to everyone looking to trade on Nasdaq. Island is set up to handle an enormous volume of trades and displays some of the leading technology behind direct access to the markets. Island opens at approximately 8:00 A.M. Eastern Time every day that the Nasdaq is open and closes approximately 1 hour and 15 minutes after the close of trading, based on subscriber demand.

Instinet. Instinet, a Reuters company, likes to refer to itself as the world's largest agency brokerage firm instead of as an ECN. Instinet allows its users to trade in over 40 markets 24 hours a day and to reduce trading and transaction costs by interacting directly with each other. Instinet historically has served institutional brokers only, but it is now making its way toward serving the individual investor as well.

REDIBook. The REDIBook ECN, developed by Speer, Leeds & Kellogg in connection with its proprietary computer interface REDIPlus, brings together the order flow of several Wall Street firms in order to provide a greater number of active buyers and sellers, thus a more efficient market. The REDIBook ECN also offers after-hours trading for selected NYSE and Amex stocks up until 10:00 P.M. Eastern Time.

Other ECNs. There are a number of other ECNs in existence, such as Bloomberg's Tradebook, Strike, Brut, and NexTrade. The major factor when determining which ECN to use is the volume levels. Remember that ECNs are essentially order books, and they need volume in order to be able to efficiently match buyers and sellers.

The ECNs described in this chapter are some of the most active ECNs at this point in time. As technology is changing so quickly, it is very possible that new players could emerge or that we could see the combination of major institutions and groups forming their own ECN. It is important to remember that each ECN requires different hardware and software. Because the ECN industry is so new, it is best to access the ECNs through your online broker, as they will have created an Internet interface to simplify the process. As direct access to the markets continues to develop, ECNs will gain in popularity among the online investors. There will eventually be a handful of ECNs that handle the majority of the traffic, much the same way it is now. However, the online brokerages and ECNs that create the most easy-to-use interface will be the big winners with the millions of online investors out there who get into electronic trading.

THE FUTURE

Online brokerage firms are scrambling to create a need for their services in the marketplace so that they do not become bypassed by execution services that eliminate the middleman and join buyers and sellers directly. Because the world's financial markets are heading toward a direct model, the online brokerages will be the ones to create an easy-to-use interface and hold the hands of investors as they begin to use this new technology. Especially with their investments in developing ECNs, brokerages are preparing themselves to offer online investors another level of information and execution that provides them with the best tools available to anyone.

After-hours trading is the first stage of new investing technology for online investors. Eventually more and more individuals will begin to access the world's financial markets at any time, day or night. Until then, because there are not as many buyers and sellers in the markets after normal market hours, it is a tool that is used by more advanced and/or active traders. In the future we will also use after-hours trading technology in order to get a more in-depth look at who is trading a particular stock and trade directly with another party. Eventually there will be no such thing as after-hours trading because the markets will always be open for everyone to trade directly with another party in any part of the world.

MAIN POINTS TO REMEMBER

- After-hours trading allows online investors to take advantage of news that breaks after the market closes and to buy or sell a stock.
- The rules for after-hours trading are different than normal online investing.
- After-hours trading tends to involve greater market fluctuations and risks than normal online investing.
- The technology behind after-hours trading will eventually allow individuals to trade directly with another party at any time, day or night.

C H A P T E R

9

RESOURCES AVAILABLE ONLINE

INFORMATION AVAILABLE ONLINE

There is enough information available on the Internet about online investing to keep you reading for a century. The key is to know the best places to go and what information is pertinent to your needs. Although there are hundreds of web sites devoted to online investing and personal finance in general, there are certain ones that are head and shoulders above the rest. In this chapter we walk you through some of the best sites devoted to the online investor and highlight their key features. Each of these sites can provide you with as much or as little information as you need to manage your portfolio. Most even have a customization tool so that every time you go back to the site you can look at your portfolio and get any news on your stocks, all in one place. Spend some time on the following sites; then decide which ones best suit your needs.

CBS MarketWatch
www.cbsmarketwatch.com

CBS MarketWatch (Figure 9-1) is a good overall site for online investors and has several basic categories including news, commentary, and personal finance. It is a great resource for the day's latest news, as well as insider insight on what shifts within the market will mean. Its content is more suited toward intermediate and advanced investors and offers clean, concise information.

The Market Data section is a great place to get the latest information on what's happening in the stock market. This area includes information on mutual funds, bonds, currencies, global markets, futures, and overall market research. It is also a great place to chart market patterns and find out about the latest earnings headlines. The Research Center offers annual reports as well as conference call audio replays. This area also offers a complete list of recent IPO filings, an area of interest to many investors lately, what with the active IPO market. The Global Market section is also of help to those with international investments, providing the indices on the markets of the Americas, Asia, Europe, Africa, and the Middle East.

CBS MarketWatch features a Personal Portfolio section where you can track the individual stocks within your portfolio. The site asks you to register and input the stocks you have purchased, at what cost, when, and your exit strategy. Registration is free, and although the site asks a few personal questions, it is relatively impersonal and is mostly being collected for demographic information the site can report to current and potential investors and advertisers. It's a great way to check on your investments as often as you like and monitor the progress of your portfolio. (It should be noted that other sites also offer this customizable service, including The

Motley Fool and Yahoo Finance). The Personal Finance area offers information ranging from real estate, retirement, tax information, and content oriented to the small business owner. This last section is great and not found on every finance site. It includes a wide range of information on subjects such as charity, advertising, and legal matters. There is also a Reference Desk in the Personal Finance area that helps the user navigate the site more effectively.

CBS MarketWatch does a very good job offering commentary on a variety of different subjects, with writers holding widely differing opinions. Although no one has all the answers, it is interesting to read columns by writers who have experience writing from print heavyweights such as *Fortune* and *Money.* Marshall Loeb is also a great resource here, writing a column called "Your Dollars" and covering subjects ranging from municipal bonds and financial aid for college to how to set your kids up comfortably in their retirement. Another interesting and decidedly one of the more amusing writers is Zapman. Offering editorial opinion that is "intended to be investment advice," Zapman remains an anonymous personality who spouts his opinion about different topics. Perhaps most amusing is the fact that above each article, where there should be a picture of the author, there is simply a shot of a person with a bag over his head. Overall, CBS MarketWatch offers a wide variety of content that represents an excellent resource for online investors.

Hoover's
www.hoovers.com

Hoover's (Figures 9-2 through 9-6) is one of the best places for public company information on the Internet. The site is easy to use and geared toward all investors. Hoover's has a wealth of information available for free on every public company and allows users to access SEC filings and annual reports. Hoover's offers a premium service that enables users to access expanded company information and real-time SEC filings. However, the free content is more than enough to get started and make the most out of what is available on

Figure 9-1. *(Courtesy of CBS.MarketWatch.com)*

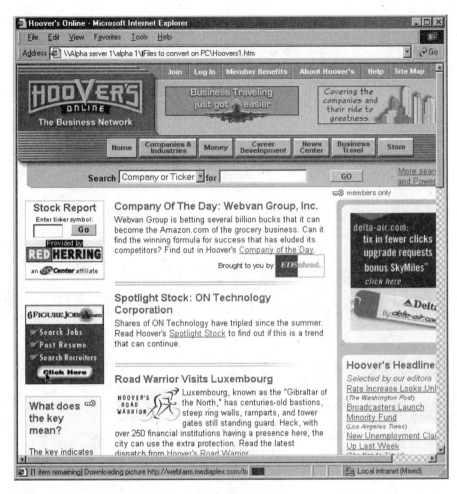

Figure 9-2. *(Courtesy of Hoover's Online, www.hoovers.com)*

Figure 9-3. *(Courtesy of Hoover's Online, www.hoovers.com)*

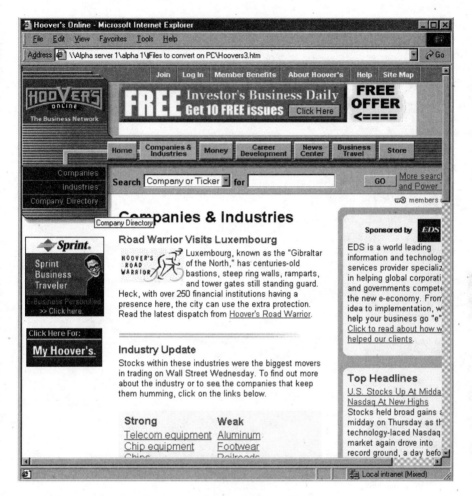

Figure 9-4. *(Courtesy of Hoover's Online, www.hoovers.com)*

Figure 9-5. *(Courtesy of Hoover's Online, www.hoovers.com)*

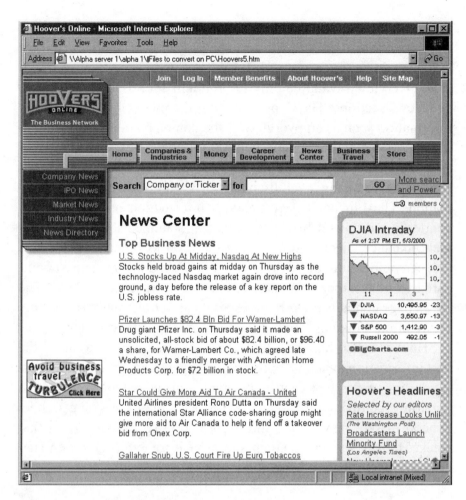

Figure 9-6. *(Courtesy of Hoover's Online, www.hoovers.com)*

the site.

Hoover's allows the user to see a group of stocks within a particular industry or sector. It breaks out its information into Capsule, Overview (available only to premium subscribers), Financial, and News sections. The Capsule page is the main page and includes information such as an overview of the company, main competitors, officers of the company, and number of employees. The Overview page contains a much more detailed overview of the company, officers of the company, overall competitors, and other pertinent information. The Financial page contains information on a company's quarterly and annual historical financial statements (income statement, balance sheet, and cash flow) as well as other market ratios that can help you understand how a stock has done in the past compared to other stocks, industries, and the market as a whole. The News page contains press releases and search functions to find other information "floating" around the Web on a specific company.

Hoover's also has the IPO Corner, which contains some of the best information available online regarding upcoming and past IPOs. If you sign up for the free weekly email, you can receive information regarding companies that have announced they are going public, general market news, and other information specifically from that week. Hoover's is an excellent site to visit for information on specific companies and to learn about industries in general.

InvestorGuide.com
www.investorguide.com

InvestorGuide.com's (Figures 9-7 through 9-9) mission is to give its users complete control over their financial future. InvestorGuide.com personally visits and hand-picks the thousands of investing links it lists on its site, and organizes them in a manner so that online investors can maximize their online investing experience. Together with its Investorville message boards and InvestorWords online investing glossary, it offers online investors a one-stop shop

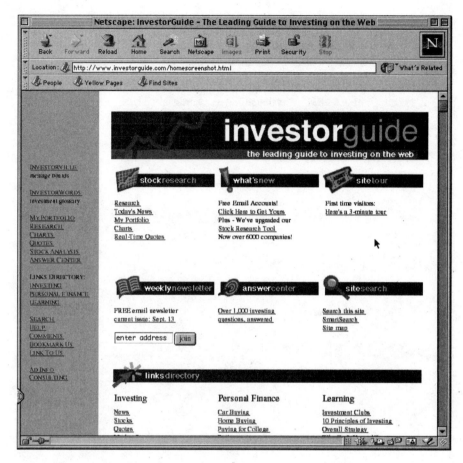

Figure 9-7. *(Courtesy of InvestorGuide.com)*

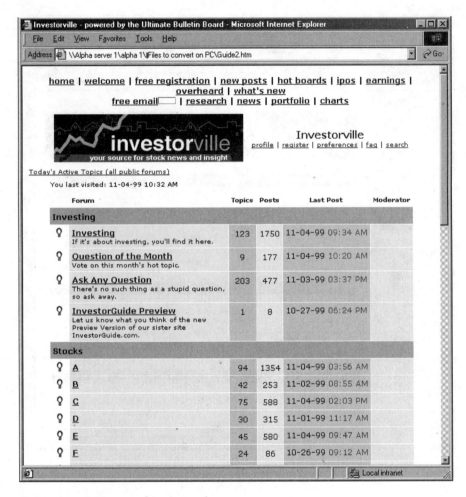

Figure 9-8. *(Courtesy of InvestorGuide.com)*

**investor**words
the biggest, best investing glossary on the web

Home | Search | Help | Suggest a Word | Bookmark | Link | NetWords
License InvestorWords | Advertise | Investorville | InvestorGuide.com

With over 5,000 definitions and 15,000 links between related terms, InvestorWords is the most comprehensive financial glossary you'll find anywhere, online or off. Just click on one of the links below to begin.

Aa-	Ad-	Al-	Ap-	At-	Ba-	Bd-	Bo-	Br-	Caa-	Cas-	Cb-	Ci-	Com
Con	Coo-	Cp-	Da-	Ded-	Di	Dj-	Ea-	En-	Ex	Fa-	Fi-	Fn-	Ga-
Gr-	H	Ia-	Ine-	Int	Inv-	J	K	La-	Li-	Maa-	Mas-	Mo-	Na-
Nf-	Ob-	Op	Or-	Pa	Pe-	Po-	Pri	Pro-	Q	Ra-	Red-	Rep-	Rh-
Sa-	See-	She-	Sta-	Str-	Ta-	Te-	Tr-	U	V	W	X	Y	Z-#

Just click here and a new window will open with our other site, InvestorGuide.com, a comprehensive guide to all the best online investing sites. This window will allow you to look up any unfamiliar words if you come across any.

Webmasters: If you operate a high-traffic financial web site and would like to have this glossary for your visitors through an arrangement similar to the E*Trade agreement, contact us about our licensing program.

First time visitor? Start here.

If you can't find what you're looking for, try using our search tool.

Click here for all the details on our advertising program.

If you have a site and you'd like your visitors to know about InvestorWords, please feel free to link to us.

Be sure to Bookmark InvestorWords, so you can reach it fast when you need it. If you are using Microsoft Explorer 5 or greater:
★ Make InvestorWords your homepage
★ Make InvestorGuide your homepage

Help us make InvestorWords more useful for you by telling us what you think of the site.

Accolades/Awards

Figure 9-9. *(Courtesy of InvestorGuide.com)*

for their investing information needs.

Whereas some investment sites target specific types of investors, InvestorGuide.com is appropriate for people who want to take control of their investments and personal finances. Its demographic includes everyone from the beginner who just received his first savings bond, to the expert who, on her own, just completed her fourth carefully researched online trade of the day. It provides ways for every investor to take that first step, and then guides him or her toward the completion of whatever investing goals he or she has.

InvestorGuide.com believes that every investor, regardless of experience, can benefit from a guide designed to help him or her sift through all of the investing information on the Internet. Sections that benefit everyone equally are those covering online brokers, stock information, and a comprehensive list of publicly traded companies (including home pages, research, and discussion). Although the entire site is accessible to everyone, different parts of the site are tailored for specific levels of experience. Specifically for beginners is an extensive Education Center, covering everything from getting started and the basics to investing strategies. For the truly young, the Kids and Money section provides children with a focused guide to investing online. For intermediate investors, the Extensive Research section as well as the news, portfolio, charting, and quote tools are essential. For advanced investors who may not need as much hand-holding as others, InvestorGuide.com offers some unique sections focusing on technical aspects of investing, the far-reaching effects of the economy, the increasingly interdependent global environment, and even the well-known strategies of famed investors such as Warren Buffett. InvestorGuide.com provides an excellent guide for investors to truly take advantage of all aspects of online investing.

Quote.com
www.quote.com
With the explosion of resources available on the Internet today, anyone can access the information needed to effectively manage his or her

> STREAMING CHARTS
Monitor your portfolio, tick by tick. Detach them from the application and keep them on your desktop all day!

> STREAMING STOCK TICKER
Easy-to-use and read Java stock ticker, listed by company logo or symbol.

> FULLY CUSTOMIZABLE WEBSITE
Over 40 customizable features from nine different categories—quotes, streaming charts, streaming stock ticker, stock portfolios, real-time news, hot lists, market research page layouts, and more — for the ultimate personalized investment experience.

> EXCLUSIVE NEWS CENTER
Let the Quote.com News team keep you up to date on the latest market-moving news. Also, get news targeted to your portfolio. Even get updates e-mailed to you.

> EMAIL ALERTS
Receive email alerts throughout the day alerting you to any news that affects your holdings, with latest prices for your holdings.

(continued on the back)

Figure 9-10. *(Courtesy of Quote.com)*

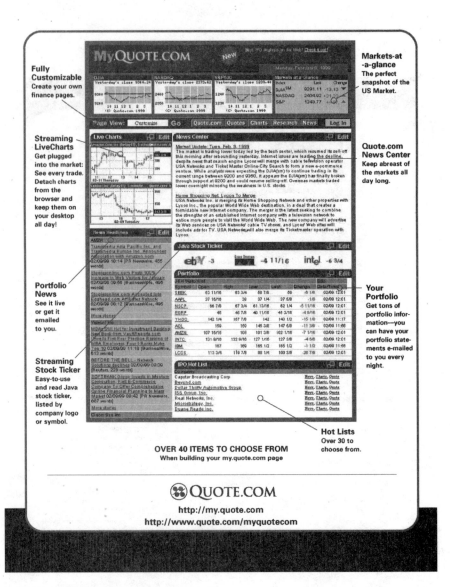

Figure 9-11. *(Courtesy of Quote.com)*

QUOTE.COM

QUOTE.COM IS THE NETWORK FOR THE INVESTING revolution. As an internet pioneer Quote.com has grown from its launch in 1994 to a site that now has more than 330,000 registered users. Quote.com provides quotes and charting on stocks, options, indices, commodity futures and mutual funds. In addition to comprehensive proprietary charting Quote.com also supplies news, earnings, research, fundamentals, and insider trading from assorted Wall Street sources, including Dow Jones, Reuters, MarketGuide, and First Call.

Quote.com began as a ground breaking Web site with the goal of creating the single best source of financial market information on the Internet. Quote.com listens to the needs and demands of online investors, and addresses those needs with constant product develoment. In 1997 Quote.com released LIVE!Charts, the first streaming Java-based charts on the Web. In June 1998 Quote.com expanded into a Windows-environment with QCharts, a real-time financial desktop application which runs over the Internet. December 1998 saw the release of IPO Edge, an exclusive pre- and post-IPO rating and analysis service, followed by the releases of My.Quote.com and the Investor Education center in early 1999.

(continued on the back)

Figure 9-12. *(Courtesy of Quote.com)*

Quote.Coms expertise as a complete financial site is recognized by the nations top financial institutions, media companies, and non-financial corporations who choose to partner with Quote.com to deliver news, market information, and analytical tools to their customers. Quote.com currently works with more than 300 partners.

QUOTE.COM
At-a-glance updates on industry news, market indices, economic indicators, free quotes and more!

QCHARTS
Hot Lists, quote sheets, embedded browsers and streaming charts!

MY.QUOTE.COM
Create your own totally customizable financial home page, with streaming charts and ticker symbols, your portfolio, portfolio analysis, news and more!

LIVE! CHARTS
Streaming Java-based applet tracks market changes as they occur-no delays, no screen refreshing!

IPO EDGE
Generate Insight™ and Foresight™ reports using data from IPO Crossroads™ proprietary database!

INVESTOR EDUCATION CENTER
How do I roll over my 401K? What is a delayed opening on the NYSE? How do I get started investing online? Learn all of this and more from the experts at Quote.com!

✪ QUOTE.COM

www.quote.com
The network for the investing revolution

850 North Shoreline Boulevard Mountain View, CA 94043-1931
tel 650.930.1000 fax 650.930.1111

Information subject to change. For the latest product and company information, visit our website at www.quote.com. 6/99

Figure 9-12 continued.   *(Courtesy of Quote.com)*

QCharts

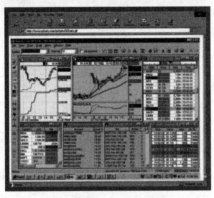

QCHARTS PROVIDES INSTANT ACCESS TO REAL-TIME financial information enabling you to make fast, profitable investment decisions. You'll have the entire market at your fingertips, whether you're in the office, at home, or on the road!

On any desktop, QCharts equips investors with live updated charts, quote sheets, hot lists, historical time and sales data, and summary period data. A built-in web browser supplies Quote.com fundamental information about individual securities, as well as up-to-the-minute news. These features can be combined to create custom workspaces tailored to your individual investment style and preferences. QCharts provides the instant access to real-time financial information you need to help your clients — and you — make investment decisions. It puts a world of financial information at your fingertips whether you're in the office or on the road. Ultra-fast and breathtakingly easy to set up and use, QCharts transforms your desktop in seconds into a state-of-the-art trading station. Whether your e working on a 28.8 kpbs modem or on the company network, QCharts puts you in the market by keeping you up-to-the-moment as the market changes.

(continued on the back)

> **NASDAQ LEVEL II**
View the best bid/ask for all market makers at Nasdaq and all regional exchanges for listed stocks, number of shares available at each price level, buying and selling pressure for a stock, up/down ticks.

> **CHARTS**
Display any time interval—from tick-by-tick, to n-minute intra-day bars to yearly—with technical analysis and up to ten years of historical data downloaded in an instant.

> **HOT LISTS**
Continuously-updated "top 10" lists of symbols, most active, suddenly active, unclosed gaps, etc. Short-term and long-term indicators

Figure 9-13. *(Courtesy of Quote.com)*

QCharts Features and Benefits

Nasdaq Level II—View the best bid/ask for all market makers at Nasdaq and all regional exchanges for listed stocks, including number of shares available at each price level, buying and selling pressure for a stock, and up/down ticks; track market makers with Market Maker I.D. Tracker

Real-Time Charting—Intraday Tick by Tick Streaming Charts and Historical Charts with 10 years of history, including volume

Speed—Utilizing proprietary Continuum Technology, QCharts is able to provide speed comparable to a T1 over the Internet

Portfolios—Create unlimited personal portfolios and customize the tables by last, change, high, low, net, volume and then sort by the column of your choice

News—Co-mingled Full-Text News stories from Dow Jones, Reuters, Business Wire, Associated Press, PR Newswire and many others

Affordable—With Professional Rates, Volume Discounts and our internet accessibility which erases the need for dedicated phone lines or satellites, QCharts is one of the most cost efficient information systems available

Personal Alerts—Create unlimited lists of alerts for stocks, options, mutual funds, based on price, volume, 52 Week highs/lows

Reliability—QCharts is a Windows-based stand-alone application, which is not affected by browser instabilities

Time & Sales—Over two years of complete time & sales history—longer then any other information provider. Filter by Size, Volume (Block/Non Block), and Type of Trade. Includes all corrected and cancelled trades. Allows you to check and confirm execution for the last year and a half

Hot Lists—Scans the market for you finding Most Active, Unusual Volume, Percent Gainers and Losers. Provides an overall feel for the market and generates buy and sell ideas

Technical Analysis—Candle, Bar, Lognormal to determine trend so that you can make market timing decisions

Charts—Candle, Bar, Lognormal to determine trend so that you can make market timing decisions

Customizable Windows—Create and Save Personal Workspaces customized to the specific portfolios, market indicators, news and charting information preferred

Complete Fundamentals—Full Fundamental coverage, with additional information from S&P Market Guide and Baseline

Complete Fundamentals—Full Fundamental coverage, including advanced company reports and balance sheet information

SEC Filings—Complete Edgar Online Filings

Insider Trading—Full Coverage to follow Insider Trading Transactions

Earnings Estimates—Full Earnings Estimates providing timely earnings estimates and Buy/Sell/Hold recommendations

Market Watch—Follow the markets by geographic location with CityWatch, or by Market Sector with the IndustryWatch, Intraday lists of stocks hitting their 52 week Highs/Lows will assist in evaluating current market conditions

Full Option Analysis—Implied Volatilities, Option Chains

Technical Analysis Studies—Including Bollinger Bands, Donchian Channels, Price Envelopes, Choppiness Index, Directional Movement (ADX), MACD, Momentum, Rate of Change, Relative Strength Index, Stochastic, Volume, Open Interest, and On Balance Volume

Technical Charting Tools—Trend lines and retracement

> **TIME AND SALES**
On-demand access to complete trade and bid/ask history, filter by type of trade, size, or price, color-coding indicates type of quote or exchange correction

> **QUOTE SHEETS**
Create and monitor portfolios for each of your customers, view hundreds or thousands of instruments at once, customizable fields and columns, unlimited customizable alerts

> **PORTFOLIOS**
Unlimited personal portfolios and customized tables

⊗ QUOTE.COM
www.quote.com
The network for the investing revolution

850 North Shoreline Boulevard Mountain View, CA 94043-1931
tel 650.930.1000 fax 650.930.1111

Figure 9-13 continued.   *(Courtesy of Quote.com)*

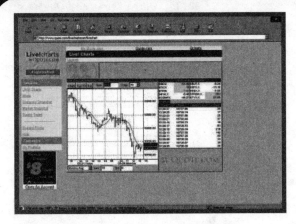
> Lightning-fast performance

> Crisp charts (one minute up to quarterly) & portfolios

> Market-moving Hot Lists, time and sales, and more

> Online tick by tick data—*every trade*

> Latest news, company research & fundamental data

> Technical Studies— moving averages, MACD, stochastics, and more!

LIVECHARTS.COM IS BROUGHT TO YOU by Quote.com, bringing you the financial information you need to make fast and profitable investment decisions. Go directly to www.livecharts.com for charting, streaming ticker symbols, and markets at-a-glance. With LiveCharts you can customize to your own preferences and link directly to the Quote.com home page for news, company research, and fundamental information.

Lightning-fast streaming charts

LiveCharts puts you in the market. Lightning-fast charts and the exclusive LiveCharts Hot Lists mean that youll miss fewer opportunities—and uncover many new opportunities.

LiveCharts uses the Internet to deliver ultra-fast streaming charts. You never need to click the reload button! Both real-time and delayed exchange data are available.

LiveCharts uses the tools you already have: your Internet connection and a browser. There is nothing to download and no software to upgrade!

LiveCharts is about the size of a banner advertisement, so it loads quickly. Once loaded, switching from chart to chart takes less than a second.

Chart any North American stock or

(continued on the back)

Figure 9-14. *(Courtesy of Quote.com)*

futures contract. Charts stream as they do on professional Wall Street workstations. Every trade flashes by. Chart any interval, from one minute up to quarterly.

Hot Lists keep you plugged in to the market

Streaming Hot Lists keep you in touch with the market. Hot Lists include Point Gainers & Losers, % Gainers & Losers, Very Short Term Up & Down, Most Volatile Stocks, Unusual Volume Movers, and many more.

One click access to news, fundamentals, and research

LiveCharts is linked to Quote.com's Wall Street-quality news and company research and fundamental information including Earnings Estimates, SEC filings, Insider Trade Information, the Quote.com IPO Center, the Quote.com Mutual Fund Center & Screener, Company Profiles and Detailed Financials, and much more.

Access to your portfolio

Store your portfolio or personal "watch list." You're one click away from changing your LiveCharts stock symbol.

Equity Trader

Equity Trader is one of the Internets most useful stock evaluation tools. Using John Bollinger's proprietary model, stocks are rated according to current and future prospects for performance. In addition, stocks are rated against their industry groups. The industry groups are also rated for current and future prospects, allowing users to easily compare ratings of stocks vs their industry peer groups. Unique "Christmas tree" lights make the ratings very easy to read.

LiveCharts is Wall Street-Quality information

LiveCharts provides everything you need to track the market like an insider. Internet technology enables this streaming chart system that works like the systems on Wall Street—and its fast, reliable, and easy to use.

COMPANY RESEARCH
View company financials and earnings announcements, business summary, ratios and statistics at-a-glance

MARKET SNAPSHOT
View 52-week highs and lows for all the major US market exchanges

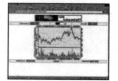

EQUITY TRADER
Rate stocks and industry groups according to current and future prospects for performance

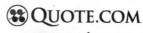

🞚 QUOTE.COM

www.quote.com
The network for the investing revolution

850 North Shoreline Boulevard Mountain View, CA 94043-1931
tel 650.930.1000 fax 650.930.1111

Figure 9-14 continued. *(Courtesy of Quote.com)*

IPO Edge

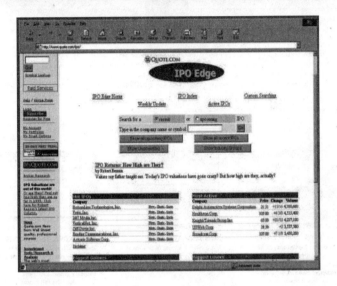

BROUGHT TO YOU EXCLUSIVELY BY QUOTE.COM. IPO Edge gives independent investors a wealth of in-depth information and analysis on the IPO market. Historically, Initial Public Offerings have been an investment sector where few people have been able to get reliable information. Underwriters have traditionally been the source for information on the companies that were going public and it was only their clients that benefitted. Now Quote.com has created the best tool on the web for YOU to research and analyze the IPO Market.

Quote.com relies on a unique combination of data and analysis that sets IPO Edge apart in its ability to provide a distinct advantage in the IPO investment environment. IPO Edge tracks companies from the announcement of their initial public offering through the period during which the offering goes into effect, and then for 18 months as a publicly traded firm.   (continued on the back)

Figure 9-15. *(Courtesy of Quote.com)*

Real-Time Reporting—Quote.coms IPO Edge provides dynamic IPO Hot lists, which include- Most Active, Daily Hot Picks, Biggest Gainers, Biggest Losers, Daily Pricings and Daily Filings. Just click on any company to get a full IPO Crossroads report and recommendation.

IPO Edge Index—Watch the IPO Edge index and historical chart, over 700 newly public companies weighted by Market Capitalization (shares x price), to get an indication of how this markets performance compares to the NASDAQ composite.

Advanced Custom Searching—Search for companies that have recently filed to go public or are newly public (up to 18 months) using name, industry group, underwriter, rating, date and many more fields. Then, view IPO Crossroads full report and recommendation on each company.

IPO Edge Reports—IPO Foresight generates an investment rating for any company that is currently in registration to go public. The investment rating is based on the IPO deal components and the past performance of similar companies. IPO Insight generates a 30-day technical rating for any company that has gone public within the previous 18 months. The rating is based on our five technical factors: Sentiment Factor, Fundamentals Factor, Market Factor, Size Factor and Deal Factor.

Greenlight Report—A daily service that delivers a company summary, pricing information and the most up-to-date annual financials for recent IPO registrations and offerings.

Learn the IPO Basics—The IPO Edge provides basic terms and fundamentals for investing in Initial Public Offerings. How important is the Underwriter in the first 6 months? What is a Greenshoe or Flipping and how does it effect you?

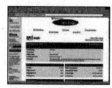  

REPORTS
Review in-depth reports with ratings recommendations, underwriter performance, financials and much more! Easily view a quote, chart or news on the same company.

MOST ACTIVE IPOs
At-a-glance listing of the most active IPOs. Drill down deeper to find out more!

ADVANCED SEARCHING
Use the IPO Edge database to search for companies by name, ticker symbol, underwriter, industry group and more. Then, view the full report with just one click.

⊗ QUOTE.COM

www.quote.com
The network for the investing revolution

850 North Shoreline Boulevard Mountain View, CA 94043-1931
tel 650.930.1000 fax 650.930.1111

Information subject to change. For the latest product and company information, visit our website at www.quote.com. 6/99
©1999 Quote.com, Inc. All rights reserved.

Figure 9-15 continued.   *(Courtesy of Quote.com)*

own investments. Quote.com (Figures 9-10 through 9-15) puts power back into the hands of people by giving them the knowledge and the tools they need so that they can break away from being solely dependent on a professional money manager to handle their investments. With Quote.com, investors have the knowledge to make their own decisions, without relying solely on advice from a third party. Quote.com offers the basics for beginners—portfolio management, news, and charts—and the services scale up from there all the way to a robust, real-time streaming market analysis and transaction tool called QCharts.

One of the extremely useful aspects of the site is the IPO Edge, a service that offers a wealth of information on IPOs. It contains information on the most recent filings, the biggest IPO gainers in the market (as well as the biggest losers), and the upcoming "Hot IPOs." For an investor specifically interested in IPOs, this is a great area to find out the latest news on companies going public.

Quote.com has a wealth of free news, charts, and portfolio management services available to any user. My.Quote.com is its fully customizable financial home page, which allows users to track their stocks and set up the page how they want to see it. Once users become more sophisticated and want to see more, they can investigate Quote.com's subscription packages that provide more news services, alerts, and real-time data.

Microsoft MoneyCentral
www.moneycentral.msn.com

MoneyCentral (Figures 9-16 through 9-19) offers a wide variety of investment information in a very easy-to-understand format. It focuses on everything from saving for college to planning for retirement in order to help individuals achieve their financial goals. MoneyCentral specifically covers topics such as Market News, Saving and Spending, Banking and Bills, Family and College, Retirement and Wills, Taxes, Insurance, and Real Estate. They have recently allowed access to premium investment services that are now free to Internet users.

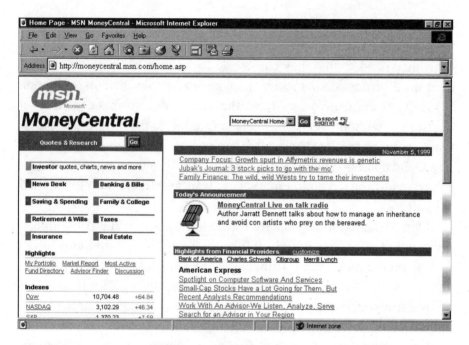

Figure 9-16. *(Courtesy of MSN Money Central)*

The best part of the MoneyCentral site is that the areas are broken out very clearly for the user. Instead of just having a Personal Finance area like many other personal finance sites, and housing every section of financial information under the same shared roof, MoneyCentral separates them, helping users to more easily and quickly arrive where they want to go on the site. Banking and Bills is probably the best section and offers information on credit cards and bank fees as well as a columnist who not only answers individual questions but also takes an active role in the corresponding message boards. The Saving and Spending area includes material as varied as whether to lease or buy a car and how to buy wine online. The "saving" in this section really refers to how to save money on individual purchases (like how to find a bargain) rather than savings account–type saving information. And this a good time to reflect on

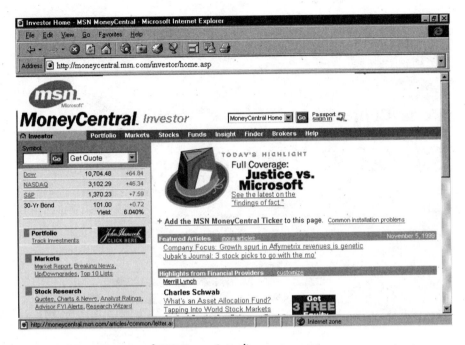

Figure 9-17. *(Courtesy of MSN Money Central)*

how smart Microsoft is, for this section also links to its Deals and Steals area, where you can see an item on sale (such as a Thanksgiving Bouquet from FTD) and click to purchase it.

Although the site is geared more toward beginner users, it contains a wealth of information that can be a great starting point for online investors. Because it is part of the Microsoft network, the site also advises you on other great sites on the Internet for all of your needs.

The Motley Fool
www.fool.com

Known for its best-selling books, The Motley Fool (Figures 9-20 through 9-24) is one of the best places to start in the quest to invest online. The web site is filled with an intelligent, tongue-in-cheek

Figure 9-18.   *(Courtesy of MSN Money Central)*

style, making it excessively easy to read and one of the few areas for investment advice that can actually be fun to read. While its message is a more general one aiming to "educate, amuse and enrich the individual investor," the Fool (as its regular users refer to it) is an epicenter for helpful, educational information about investing online and investments in general that is easy to understand and useful for all.

The site includes several outstanding features that help set it apart from the rest. First, new users are recommended to visit "The 13 Steps to Investing Foolishly." Although this area starts off with elementary investing suggestions (Step 1 tells the user to pay off debt before trying to run with the bulls and the bears), the later steps offer helpful advice such as getting an online broker (wherein it specifically lays out the costs saved for the individual investor), and addi-

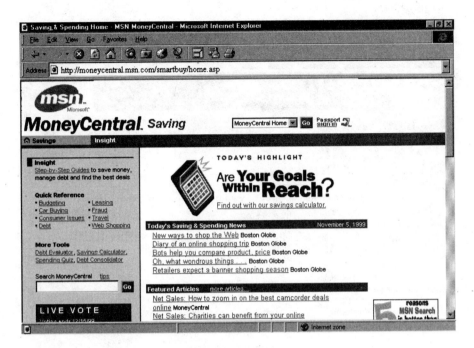

Figure 9-19.   *(Courtesy of MSN Money Central)*

tional steps about more advanced investment approaches. For those both new to the online world or new to investing, this area is a gem unlike anything else available online (and it's free).

Another shining star on The Motley Fool is the Strategies area. This section offers the user a sneak peak into several different portfolios, each with a different strategy. The Rule Breaker Portfolio, managed by David Gardner, invests in stocks based on five principles. These are specifically broken out for the user and explained in detail so that the user can understand why certain stocks are traded within the portfolio. They include, for this specific portfolio, tenets such as taking on high levels of risk and paying little attention to market history. By the way, users should note that the portfolio managers have put their money where their mouth is, taking real money

Figure 9-20. *(Courtesy of The Motley Fool, Inc., www.fool.com)*

Figure 9-21. *(Courtesy of The Motley Fool, Inc., www.fool.com)*

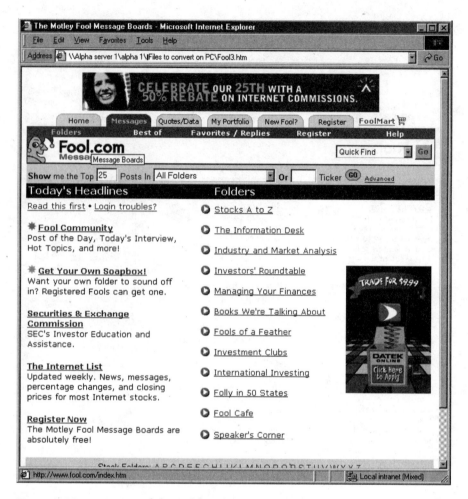

Figure 9-22. *(Courtesy of The Motley Fool, Inc., www.fool.com)*

and making the same buys they discuss on paper. Users are asked to observe the investment choices the Fools make and understand the homework that went into making these decisions. They tell users their specific buys, however, so there is certainly a segment of the audience that will simply buy what they buy when they buy, know-

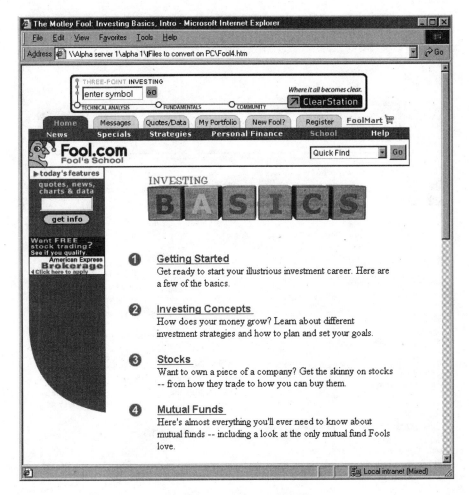

Figure 9-23. *(Courtesy of The Motley Fool, Inc., www.fool.com)*

ing their past success. As the Motley Fool would say, this is terribly unFoolish.

Another fabulous resource The Motley Fool offers is its message boards. The Motley Fool is an old timer in the Internet space; they originated as message boards on AOL's proprietary service back

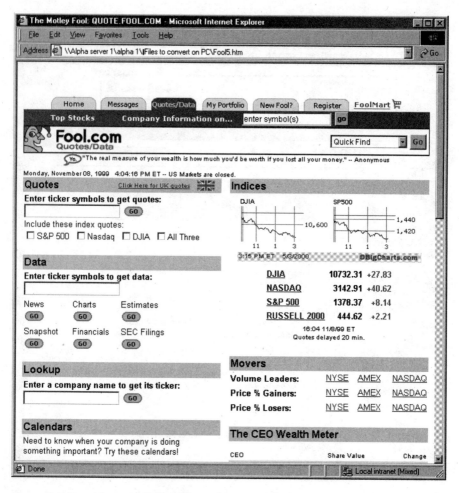

Figure 9-24. *(Courtesy of The Motley Fool, Inc., www.fool.com)*

when the Internet was just developing. AOL then asked The Motley Fool to contribute content to their service, which officially started the beginnings of The Motley Fool web site. But they remember their roots; The Fools were first known for their message boards, and they remain a shining example of what community means online. The content on these boards ranges from stock-specific advice and insight to support areas for investment clubs to debate about whether to lease or buy a car. The Gardner brothers and the staff of The Motley Fool are constant and active posters on the message boards as well, offering advice and input on a variety of topics. No question is a stupid question on these boards; the atmosphere is open and supportive, and each question is approached with the same level of respect and support. It's a great area to seek information from thousands upon thousands of fellow users.

The Motley Fool is a site for all users, but is perhaps best suited to new users and those seeking insight and conversation about investments from other users. The community and the high level of readability make this site a stand-out in a crowded category of investment sites. Keep an ear out for The Fools' radio show and frequent television appearances—you'll know them by the jester caps they wear!

TheStreet.com
www.thestreet.com

One of the premier web sites for more advanced investors, TheStreet .com (Figures 9-25 through 9-26) offers excellent content and featured services. TheStreet.com content falls into two basic categories: free and premium. The free areas of the site, accessible without registration or a subscription, include the regularly updated Markets coverage and the Basics section. The premium content is available to those who have purchased a monthly, annual, or multiyear subscription or who are currently registered for its 30-day free trial. Subscription rates are $9.95 monthly or $99.95 annually. A 30-day free trial is available to all new visitors.

Figure 9-25. *(© 1999 TheStreet.com. All rights reserved.)*

TheStreet.com's large and experienced news organization provides a comprehensive range of original financial news and in-depth analysis, whereas many financial sites prefer to aggregate content from other sites. TheStreet.com publishes more than 40 original news stories and commentaries each day. It complements the objective and hard-hitting news and analysis with commentary by leading writers, including James J. Cramer, Herb Greenberg, Brenda Buttner, and Adam Lashinsky.

TheStreet.com offers financial news and information that can help each level of investor make informed decisions. For the begin-

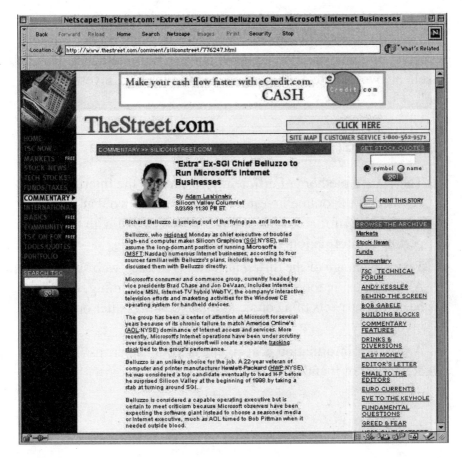

Figure 9-26.   *(© 1999 TheStreet.com. All rights reserved.)*

ner investor, it offers a helpful Basics reference section, which includes a reference library and guides that give the lowdown on topics such as mutual funds, bonds, and fundamental stock analysis. For the intermediate investor there is a Funds/Taxes section, with detailed advice and commentary on mutual funds and taxes, and the Markets section, which offers features on the world's financial markets throughout the trading day. For the advanced investor, premium stories found in the Stock News, Tech Stocks, Commentary, and International sections provide an insider's look at the world of finance.

TheStreet.com provides investors with the information they need to make informed investment decisions in addition to financial reporting and analysis that are both current and intelligent. It is an excellent overall site for intermediate to advanced investors especially.

MAIN POINTS TO REMEMBER

- There are a plethora of different web sites on the Internet devoted to the online investor. Use the one or two that you are the most comfortable with and that provides you with the most pertinent information.
- Take advantage of the different features of each web site. Although using too many sites will be overwhelming, there may be certain aspects of a couple that make you a better online investor.
- A world of information is available at your fingertips. Take advantage of it and profit from it.

GLOSSARY

10k The annual report a public company is required to file for its shareholders.

10q The quarterly report a public company is required to file for its shareholders.

Amex American Stock Exchange.

balance sheet The financial statement that lists the assets, liabilities, and shareholder's equity at a specific point in time.

bookmark A way to save a uniform resource locator (URL) for a specific web site in a folder to have fast access to it in the future.

browser Software that allows an individual to access web sites. Examples include Netscape Navigator, Microsoft Internet Explorer, and Opera.

chat   The ability to email back and forth in an instant message format.

cookies   The ability of a web site owner to track your preferences and movement within a web site.

DPOs   Direct public offerings.

DPPs   Direct purchase plans.

DRIPs   Dividend reinvestment plans.

DSL   A way to access the Internet much faster than with a normal modem line.

GTC   An order that is "good till canceled."

GTX   An order that is "good till executed."

ECN   Electronic communication network.

income statement   Financial statement that reports operating results, such as net income, for a given period.

IPO   Initial public offering; when a company offers its shares to the public.

IRA   Individual retirement account; a trust fund into which any employee can contribute up to $2,000 a year.

ISDN   Integrated services digital network; delivers information much faster than a normal phone line.

ISPs   Internet service providers; companies that provide the link that lets an individual get online. There are both local and national ISPs; the choice is up to the individual.

limit order   A broker will buy or sell the security only if the price is at a specific or better price.

market capitalization   The stock price multiplied by the number of shares outstanding. Also known as market cap.

market order   The best price available for buying or selling a stock at the time an order is received.

message boards   Available at many sites, these are like bulletin boards where users post a comment or a question and other users post responses. Message boards exist online for virtually any topic you can think of.

mutual fund   A type of investment company that invests money in a variety of stocks, bonds, options, commodities, or money market securities.

Nasdaq   National Association of Securities Dealers.

NYSE   New York Stock Exchange.

S-1   The statement a company files when it plans on going public.

SEC   Securities and Exchange Commission; the regulating body of the securities industry and exchanges.

search engine   An online robot that helps you find different web sites on the Internet. Examples include Lycos and Infoseek.

shorting   Selling a security that you do not own in the hopes that its value will decrease in price so that you can repurchase it.

SIPC   Securities Investment Protection Corporation; insurance for online brokers.

stop limit order   Used when the top price is reached or passed on a limit order.

stop order   Used to buy or sell a security once it reaches a set price.

statement of cash flow   Financial statement analyzing the changes that affect the cash account during a specific period.

T1/T3   A way to access the Internet much faster than with a normal modem line.

underwriter   The group that buys a new issue of securities from the issuing corporation and resells it to the public.

URL   Uniform resource locators; the address of a web site. It starts with "http://" and (most of the time) is followed by "www" (which stands for World Wide Web). Then comes the domain name, which includes the specific name of the site, and ".com," or ".net," or another ending that tells you where the address is located. For example, .uk is for the United Kingdom.

Index

ABOUT THE AUTHOR

Jonathan R. Aspatore is the founder of EPS Business Partners (www.epsbp.com), which provides entrepreneurial solutions to companies worldwide. He has written numerous books on entrepreneurial thinking and new business development in addition to writing a monthly column for numerous web sites and publications. Jonathan began his career with Morgan Stanley in New York after studying entrepreneurial management at the Wharton School of Business. After working as an Investment Banker in the technology sector and in the Derivatives Product Group at Morgan Stanley, he went on to start EPS Business Partners in 1997. As CEO of EPS, Jonathan has assisted numerous multimillion-dollar companies and start-ups assess and execute new business endeavors. For any comments or questions, please contact him at aspatore@epsbp.com.